'In *Cinematic Aided Design* François Penz has invented a kind of meta architecture, an imaginary Cinecitta where the production of architecture and film reflect and refract each other's gaze on the everyday. Penz casts Henri Lefebvre and Georges Perec to lead a purposely *in-disciplined* ensemble cast of film makers and architects to find our truths in the everyday space of our lives.'

– *Tom Emerson, director, 6a architects, London & professor at the Department of Architecture, ETH Zürich, Switzerland*

'In *Cinematic Aided Design*, François Penz argues persuasively that narrative cinema offers a vast library of demonstrations of architecture in use. Exploring the everyday spaces of fiction films, he identifies the essential value of moving images for architects and architecture.'

– *Patrick Keiller*

'Francois Penz is interested in what happens to architecture once it is handed over to a client, and he sees film as an accidental archive that makes visible how we live, love, work and sleep in buildings. His fascinating book offers some sparkling insights into how architects can enrich the design process with mundane knowledge. More than that, it is the best account I have read of how cinema can help us to understand the everyday.'

– *Joe Moran, Professor of English and Cultural History, Liverpool John Moores University, UK*

CINEMATIC AIDED DESIGN

Cinematic Aided Design: An Everyday Life Approach to Architecture provides architects, planners, designer practitioners, politicians and decision makers with a new awareness of the practice of everyday life through the medium of film. This novel approach will also appeal to film scholars and film practitioners with an interest in spatial and architectural issues as well as researchers from cultural studies in the field of everyday life.

The everyday life is one of the hardest things to uncover since by its very nature it remains overlooked and ignored. However, cinema has over the last 120 years represented, interpreted and portrayed hundreds of thousands of everyday life situations taking place in a wide range of dwellings, streets and cities. Film constitutes the most comprehensive lived in building data in existence. Cinema created a comprehensive encyclopedia of architectural spaces and building elements. It has exposed large fragments of our everyday life and everyday environment that this book is aiming to reveal and restitute.

Professor **François Penz** is the Head of the Department of Architecture at the University of Cambridge, a former Director of The Martin Centre for Architectural and Urban Studies and a Fellow of Darwin College. He directs the Digital Studio for Research in Design, Visualization and Communication. His current AHRC research project, 'A cinematic *musée imaginaire* of spatial cultural differences' (2017–2020), expands many of the ideas developed in this book to other cultures (China and Japan in particular), construing films of everyday life as a revelator of deep spatial cultural differences.

.

CINEMATIC AIDED DESIGN

An Everyday Life Approach to Architecture

François Penz

LONDON AND NEW YORK

First published 2018
by Routledge
2 Park Square, Milton Park, Abingdon, Oxon OX14 4RN

and by Routledge
711 Third Avenue, New York, NY 10017

Routledge is an imprint of the Taylor & Francis Group, an informa business

© 2018 François Penz

The right of François Penz to be identified as author of this work has been asserted by him in accordance with sections 77 and 78 of the Copyright, Designs and Patents Act 1988.

All rights reserved. No part of this book may be reprinted or reproduced or utilized in any form or by any electronic, mechanical, or other means, now known or hereafter invented, including photocopying and recording, or in any information storage or retrieval system, without permission in writing from the publishers.

Trademark notice: Product or corporate names may be trademarks or registered trademarks, and are used only for identification and explanation without intent to infringe.

British Library Cataloguing-in-Publication Data
A catalogue record for this book is available from the British Library

Library of Congress Cataloging-in-Publication Data
Names: Penz, Francois, author.
Title: Cinematic aided design : an everyday life approach to architecture / Francois Penz.
Description: New York : Routledge, 2017. | Includes bibliographical references and index.
Identifiers: LCCN 2017007695| ISBN 9780415639071 (hb : alk. paper) | ISBN 9780415639088 (pb : alk. paper) | ISBN 9781315722993 (ebk)
Subjects: LCSH: Motion pictures and architecture.
Classification: LCC PN1995.25 .P455 2017 | DDC 791.43/657--dc23
LC record available at https://lccn.loc.gov/2017007695

ISBN: 978-0-415-63907-1 (hbk)
ISBN: 978-0-415-63908-8 (pbk)
ISBN: 978-1-315-72299-3 (ebk)

Typeset in Sabon
by Saxon Graphics Ltd, Derby

For Fabia

CONTENTS

List of illustrations	*xi*
Filmography	*xiv*
Acknowledgements	*xix*
Introduction	1

PART 1
An everyday life approach to architecture   **9**

1   The case for everydayness   11

PART 2
Everydayness and cinema   **37**

2   Introduction to everydayness and cinema   39

3   The value of fiction and the role of disruptions   51

4   Georges Perec and Chantal Akerman   65

5   Rhythmanalysis   85

6   Cinematic typologies of everyday life and architecture   100

x Contents

PART 3
An architectonic of cinema

123

7 Introduction to an architectonic of cinema

125

8 Windows

133

9 Doors

156

10 Stairs: the invention of cinematic scalalogy

178

11 Joining the dots

198

PART 4
Cinematic aided design

217

12 Towards a cinematic approach to everyday life and architecture

219

Index

233

ILLUSTRATIONS

I.1	Film as post-occupancy study (house image by Martha Rawlinson)	4
1.1	Extract from the bibliography from Henri Lefebvre's handout (1971)	15
1.2	Extract from Henri Lefebvre's handout (1971)	15
3.1	The kitchen scene in *The Godfather* (Francis Ford Coppola, 1972)	52
3.2	Hulot in *Mon Oncle* (Jacques Tati, 1958)	54
3.3	The moment of disruption in *La Piscine* (Jacques Deray, 1969)	57
3.4	Disruption of the everyday in *Blue Velvet* (David Lynch, 1986)	58
3.5	The intrusion of the fax in *Lost in Translation* (Sofia Coppola, 2003)	59
3.6	Parallel universes in *Stunned Man* (Julian Rosefeldt, 2004)	60
4.1	*Un homme qui dort* (Bernard Queysanne, 1974): everyday life in a small place	69
4.2	*Un homme qui dort* (Bernard Queysanne, 1974): everyday scene in a Parisian bar	71
4.3	*La Chambre* (Chantal Akerman, 1972) – stills	73
4.4	*Charlotte et son Jules* (Jean-Luc Godard, 1958) – stills	74
4.5	*Jeanne Dielman* (Chantal Akerman, 1974) – kitchen planimetric shots	76
4.6	Similarities between *Jeanne Dielman* (Chantal Akerman, 1974) and *Die Neue Wohnung* (Hans Richter, 1930)	79
4.7	*Jeanne Dielman* (Chantal Akerman, 1974) – dining room planimetric shots	80
4.8	*Jeanne Dielman* (Chantal Akerman, 1974) versus *Neufert's Architects' Data*	81
5.1	The Melvin house © François Penz	89
5.2	*Exhibition* (Joanna Hogg, 2013): Start and end of Day 2	91
5.3	*Exhibition* (Joanna Hogg, 2013): the visit of the estate agents	92
5.4	*Exhibition* (Joanna Hogg, 2013): D 'pinned' against the wall	93
5.5	*Exhibition* (Joanna Hogg, 2013): empty space	95
5.6	*Exhibition* (Joanna Hogg, 2013): free plan	96

xii Illustrations

6.1	Observing the observed in *Kitchen Stories* (Bent Hamer, 2003)	101
6.2	Toast shooting scene in *Pulp Fiction* (Quentin Tarantino, 1994)	103
6.3	The oneiric house © Martha Rawlinson	106
6.4	Terraced houses in *This is My Street* (Sidney Hayers, 1964)	108
6.5	Semi-detached houses in *All the Way Up* (James MacTaggart, 1970)	110
6.6	Paterson with his dog in front of his house in *Paterson* (Jim Jarmusch, 2016)	113
6.7	*Jackie Brown* (Quentin Tarantino, 1997): a non-everyday life in an everyday environment	114
6.8	*Museum Hours* (Jem Cohen, 2012): everyday life in a non-everyday environment	115
7.1	The Elements of Architecture Venice Biennale 2014: doors	127
7.2	*Architectures d'Aujourd'hui* (Pierre Chenal, 1931): the Villa Savoye's façade	128
7.3	*House after Five Years of Living* (Charles and Ray Eames, 1955): tectonic elements	129
8.1	*Un homme qui dort* (Bernard Queysanne, 1974): practising the dormer window	134
8.2	The voyeuristic window in *Le Plaisir* (Max Ophüls, 1952)	135
8.3	The man at the window in *Damnation* (Béla Tarr, 1988)	137
8.4	The window of opportunities: *La Partie de Campagne* (Jean Renoir, 1936)	138
8.5	A world of *portes fenêtres* in *38 Témoins* (Lucas Belvaux, 2012)	143
8.6	*L'Eclisse* (Michelangelo Antonioni, 1962): Vittoria lost in window space	144
8.7	*L'Eclisse* (Michelangelo Antonioni, 1962): poster by Signac in the background	145
8.8	A typology of windows and affects in *L'Eclisse* (Michelangelo Antonioni, 1962)	146
8.9	*L'Eclisse* (Michelangelo Antonioni, 1962): window across the courtyard	147
8.10	Window onto the street in *L'Avventura* (Michelangelo Antonioni, 1960)	150
9.1	Tor struggling through doors in *Ed Wood* (Tim Burton, 1994)	157
9.2	Doors that unite and separate in *Amélie* (Jean-Pierre Jeunet, 2001)	158
9.3	Doors as mental state in *Spellbound* (Alfred Hitchcock, 1945)	159
9.4	Revolving door in *Traces* (Ches Hardy et al, 2008)	161
9.5	Riggan stuck in a door in *Birdman* (Alejandro G. Iñárritu, 2014)	162
9.6	The door as a cut: *The Servant* (Joseph Losey, 1963)	163
9.7	Doors linking time and space across the city in *Ed Wood* (Tim Burton, 1994)	164
9.8	The 'Bluebeard' door in *Rebecca* (Alfred Hitchcock, 1940)	167
9.9	The door that reveals in *The Servant* (Joseph Losey, 1963)	168
9.10	Inhabiting the threshold in *L'Eclisse* (Michelangelo Antonioni, 1962)	169
9.11	Opening onto a private world in *Two Days One Night* (Dardenne brothers, 2014)	171
9.12	'Honey, I'm home' in *The Shining* (Stanley Kubrick, 1980)	172
10.1	D hugging the staircase in *Exhibition* (Joanna Hogg, 2013)	180

10.2	Handrails in *Night of the Demon* (Jacques Tourneur, 1957) and technical detail	181
10.3	Detective Arbogast falling backwards down a straight staircase n *Psycho* (Alfred Hitchcock, 1960)	182
10.4	Tati challenging Blondel's formula in *Cours du Soir par Jacques Tati* (Nicolas Rybowski, 1967)	183
10.5	Spiral staircases in *Alphaville* (Jean-Luc Godard, 1966)	184
10.6	'L'ai-je bien descendu?' in *Alphaville* (Jean-Luc Godard, 1966)	185
10.7	The Odessa steps in *Battleship Potemkin* (Sergei Eisenstein, 1925)	187
10.8	Hulot's climb in *Mon Oncle* (Jacques Tati, 1958)	188
10.9	*Ballet Mécanique* (Fernand Léger, 1924): the steps of everyday life	190
10.10	Staircase scene in *Gone with the Wind* (Victor Fleming, 1939)	191
10.11	The ambiguous stairs in *Le Révélateur* (Philippe Garrel, 1968)	193
10.12	Going down in *Psycho* (Alfred Hitchcock, 1960)	194
11.1	Inhabiting staircases in *Delicatessen* (Jean-Pierre Jeunet and Marc Caro, 1991)	199
11.2	The lift in *Pulp Fiction* (Quentin Tarantino, 1994)	201
11.3	The corridor as 'retarder' in *Pulp Fiction* (Quentin Tarantino, 1994)	203
11.4	*Le Mépris* (Jean-Luc Godard, 1963): the unfinished flat	207
11.5	The statue in *Le Mépris* (Jean-Luc Godard, 1963)	208
11.6	Doors as gaps between walls in *Le Mépris* (Jean-Luc Godard, 1963)	209
11.7	Walls as 'emotional condensers' in *Le Mépris* (Jean-Luc Godard, 1963)	210
11.8	The door with no middle in *Le Mépris* (Jean-Luc Godard, 1963)	211
11.9	Inhabiting corners in *Le Mépris* (Jean-Luc Godard, 1963)	213
11.10	Camille going down the staircase in *Le Mépris* (Jean-Luc Godard, 1963)	213
12.1	Closing the loop (house image by Martha Rawlinson)	219
12.2	Café scene in *The Aviator's Wife* (Eric Rohmer, 1981)	226
12.3	Café scene (1) in *Full Moon in Paris* (Eric Rohmer, 1984)	227
12.4	Café scene (2) in *Full Moon in Paris* (Eric Rohmer, 1984)	227

Plates

1	Wim Wenders talking to Sanaa Architects – a production still from *If Buildings Could Talk* © Neue Road Movies (Wim Wenders, 2010)
2	Performing domestic tasks in *Home* (Ursula Meier, 2009)
3	*Habiter l'inhabituel*, exhibition by Eric Hattan (2014)
4	The Elements of Architecture Venice Biennale 2014: windows
5	The right to light in *L'Homme d'à coté* (Gastón Duprat and Mariano Cohn, 2009)
6	*Two Days One Night*: the doors of hope and expectations (Dardenne brothers, 2014)
7	Shorthand for architecture in *Drive* (Nicolas Winding Refn, 2011)

FILMOGRAPHY

38 Témoins (Lucas Belvaux, 2012)

Abigail's Party (Mike Leigh, 1977)

A Clockwork Orange (Stanley Kubrick, 1971)

A History of Violence (David Cronenberg, 2005)

All The Way Up (James MacTaggart, 1970)

Alphaville (Jean-Luc Godard, 1966)

Amélie (Jean-Pierre Jeunet, 2001)

Another Year (Mike Leigh, 2010)

Architectures d'Aujourd'hui (Pierre Chenal, 1931)

Badlands (Terrence Malick, 1973)

Ballet Mécanique (Fernand Léger, 1924)

Battleship Potemkin (Sergei Eisenstein, 1925)

Bicycle Thieves (Vittorio De Sica, 1948)

Billy Liar (John Schlesinger, 1963)

Birdman (Alejandro G. Iñárritu, 2014)

Bleak Moments (Mike Leigh, 1971)

Blonde Venus (Josef von Sternberg, 1932)

Blue Velvet (David Lynch, 1986)

Boyhood (Richard Linklater, 2013)

Brannigan (Douglas Hickox, 1975)

Breakfast at Tiffany's (Blake Edwards, 1961)

Bringing Out the Dead (Martin Scorsese, 1999)

Charlotte et son Jules (Jean-Luc Godard, 1958)

Chevalier (Athina Rachel Tsangari, 2016)

Filmography **xv**

Chronique d'un été (Jean Rouch, 1961)

Citizen Kane (Orson Welles, 1941)

Cosh Boy (Lewis Gilbert, 1953)

Cours du Soir par Jacques Tati (Nicolas Rybowski, 1967)

Critique de la séparation (Guy Debord, 1961)

Damnation (Béla Tarr, 1988)

Delicatessen (Jean-Pierre Jeunet and Marc Caro, 1991)

Divine Intervention (Suleiman, 2002)

Dogville (Lars von Trier, 2003)

Do the Right Thing (Spike Lee, 1989)

Drive (Nicolas Winding Refn, 2011)

Ed Wood (Tim Burton, 1994)

Exhibition (Joanna Hogg, 2013)

Fahrenheit 451 (François Truffaut, 1966)

Family Life (Ken Loach, 1971)

Film (Samuel Beckett, 1965)

Fish Tank (Andrea Arnold, 2009)

Frances Ha (Noah Baumbach, 2012)

Gentleman's Agreement (Elia Kazan, 1947)

Gone with the Wind (Victor Fleming, 1939)

Helsinki, Forever (Peter von Bagh, 2008)

Her (Spike Jonze, 2013)

Hiroshima Mon Amour (Alain Resnais, 1959)

Home (Ursula Meier, 2009)

Hotel Monterey (Chantal Akerman, 1972)

House After Five Years of Living (Charles and Ray Eames, 1955)

I am Cuba (Mikhail Kalatozov, 1964)

I Confess (Alfred Hitchcock, 1953)

If Buildings Could Talk (Wim Wenders, 2010)

Jackie Brown (Quentin Tarantino, 1997)

Jeanne Dielman, 23, Quai du Commerce, 1080 Bruxelles (Chantal Akerman, 1974)

Jour de Fête (Jacques Tati, 1947)

Jules and Jim (François Truffaut, 1962)

Kill Bill 1 (Quentin Tarantino, 2003)

Kiss Me Deadly (Robert Aldrich, 1955)

Kitchen Stories (Bent Hamer, 2003)

L'Arroseur Arosé (Louis Lumière, 1895)

La Chambre (Chantal Akerman, 1972)

xvi Filmography

La Femme de l'Aviateur [The Aviator's Wife] (Eric Rohmer, 1981)

La Piscine (Jacques Deray, 1969)

La Strada (Frederico Fellini, 1954)

Late Spring (Yasujirō Ozu, 1949)

L'Avventura (Michelangelo Antonioni, 1960)

Le Crime de Monsieur Lange (Jean Renoir, 1936)

Le Jour se Lève (Marcel Carné, 1939)

Le Mépris (Jean-Luc Godard, 1963)

Le Plaisir (Max Ophüls, 1952)

Le Révélateur (Philippe Garrel, 1968)

Le Samourai (Jean-Pierre Melville, 1967)

Les convoyeurs attendent (Benoît Mariage, 1999)

Les lieux d'une fugue (Georges Perec, 1978)

Les Nuits de la Pleine Lune [Full moon in Paris] (Eric Rohmer, 1984)

L'Eclisse (Michelangelo Antonioni, 1962)

L'homme d'à coté (Gastón Duprat and Mariano Cohn, 2009)

London (Patrick Keiller, 1994)

Lost in Translation (Sofia Coppola, 2003)

Melody (Waris Hussein, 1971)

Midnight Cowboy (John Schlesinger, 1969)

Mix me a Person (Leslie Norman, 1964)

Momma Don't Allow (Karel Reisz and Tony Richardson, 1956)

Mon Oncle (Jacques Tati, 1958)

Museum Hours (Jem Cohen, 2012)

Night of the Demon (Jacques Tourneur, 1957)

Night on Earth (Jim Jarmusch, 1991)

Ninotchka (Ernst Lubitsch, 1939)

No Country for Old Men (Cohen brothers, 2007)

Nostalghia (Andrei Tarkosvky, 1983)

Notorious (Alfred Hitchcock, 1946)

Number Seventeen (Alfred Hitchcock, 1932)

O Dreamland (Lindsay Anderson, 1953)

Out of the Rubble (Penny Woolcock, 2016)

Paterson (Jim Jarmusch, 2016)

Pierrot le Fou (Jean-Luc Godard, 1965)

Playtime (Jacques Tati, 1967)

Point Break (Kathryn Bigelow, 1991)

Poor Cow (Ken Loach, 1967)

Prénom Carmen (Jean-Luc Godard, 1983)

Psycho (Alfred Hitchcock, 1960)

Pulp Fiction (Quentin Tarantino, 1994)

Ratcatcher (Lynne Ramsay, 1999)

Rear Window (Alfred Hitchcock, 1953)

Rebecca (Alfred Hitchcock, 1940)

Récits d'Ellis Island (Robert Bober and Georges Perec, 1979)

Repulsion (Roman Polanski, 1965)

Reservoir Dogs (Quentin Tarantino, 1992)

Rosemary's Baby (Roman Polanski, 1968)

Salt of the Earth (Herbert J. Biberman, 1954)

Saving Private Ryan (Steven Spielberg, 1998)

Série noire (Alain Corneau, 1979)

Spellbound (Alfred Hitchcock, 1945)

Strangers on a Train (Alfred Hitchcock, 1951)

Stunned Man (Julian Rosefeldt, 2004)

Sunset Boulevard (Billy Wilder, 1950)

The Awful Truth (Leo McCarey, 1937)

The Battle of Algiers (Gillo Pontecorvo, 1966)

The Birds (Alfred Hitchcock, 1963)

The Cameraman (Buster Keaton, 1928)

The Clock (Christian Marclay, 2010)

The Dilapidated Dwelling (Patrick Keiller, 2000)

La Ligne Générale [The General Line] (Sergei Eisenstein and Grigori Alexandrov, 1929)

The Girl Chewing Gum (John Smith, 1976)

The Godfather (Francis Ford Coppola, 1972)

The Hudsucker Proxy (Coen Brothers, 1994)

The Last Picture Show (Peter Bogdanovich, 1971)

The London Story (Sally Potter, 1986)

The Optimists of Nine Elms (Anthony Simmons, 1973)

The Passenger (Michelangelo Antonioni, 1975)

The pervert's guide to cinema by Slavoj Žižek (Sophie Fiennes, 2006)

The Pilgrim (Charlie Chaplin, 1923)

The Rink (Charlie Chaplin, 1916)

The Sacrifice (Andrei Tarkosvky, 1986)

The Servant (Joseph Losey, 1963)

The Shining (Stanley Kubrick, 1980)

The Strange Little Cat (Ramon Zürcher, 2013)

xviii Filmography

The Tina Trilogy (Penny Woolcock, 1999–2006)

The Tree of Life (Malick, USA, 2011)

The Twilight Zone (Rod Sterling, 1959)

The Wizard of Oz (Victor Fleming, 1939)

This is My Street (Sidney Hayers, 1964)

Together (Lorenza Mazzetti, 1956)

Traces (Ches Hardy et al, 2008)

Two Days One Night (Dardenne brothers, 2014)

Two or Three Things I Know About Her (Jean-Luc Godard, 1967)

Umberto D (Vittorio De Sica, 1952)

Un homme qui dort [The Man Who Sleeps] (Bernard Queysanne, 1974)

Une Partie de Campagne (Jean Renoir, 1936)

Up the Junction (Peter Collinson, 1967)

Vertical Promenade (Miguel Santa Clara, 2008)

Villain (Michael Tuchner, 1971)

West Side Story (Robert Wise and Jerome Robbins, 1961)

ACKNOWLEDGEMENTS

I wish first to acknowledge the Department of Architecture and all my colleagues for having directly or indirectly supported this project over the last three years. My association with film studies dates from the early 1990s when I met Maureen Thomas, then Head of Screen Studies at the National Film and Television School. I am immensely grateful for her continuous intellectual support, encouragement and suggestions over such a sustained period. After the demise of Cambridge University Moving Image Studio and the loss of our MPhil in Architecture and the Moving Image in 2005, the start of the interdisciplinary Screen Media and Cultures (SMaC) MPhil in 2006 provided me with a new outlet for my cinematic spatial explorations. I would like here to express my gratitude to all my colleagues from the Faculty of Modern & Medieval Languages and the Faculty of English who have provided a new home for my teaching and research. Crucially this new strand allowed me to recruit several excellent doctoral students from different disciplines, who have all contributed to shaping my thoughts, together with my past and current PhD students.

More recently I started to teach on our two new Masters in Architecture and Urban Studies [MAUS] and in Architecture and Urban Design [MAUD], allowing me to mix the film students with our architecture students. Bringing together those two strands has provided me with a new dynamic. As a result I have been privileged to work with many outstanding students whose work has contributed to my thinking. I am particularly grateful to the SMaC and MAUS cohorts of 2014–2015 and 2015–2016 who bravely elected to follow my cinematic approach to everyday life seminars, providing me with endless insightful and enjoyable conversations.

Lectures and supervisions with second- and third-year Architecture undergraduates during the last three years have been equally rewarding. Among these I wish to single out Henry Jiao and Audrey Lejeune for their wonderful dissertations, respectively on *Exhibition* (Joanna Hogg, 2013) and *Amélie* (Jean-Pierre Jeunet, 2001) – in the process, Audrey almost managed to reconcile me with *Amélie*! I also wish to thank Martha Rawlinson, whose dissertation *The House that Image Built* in 2012 unwittingly started me thinking about the everyday in a novel way. I am also very grateful to her for giving me permission to use her dissertation cover image.

I am indebted to the numerous conferences and seminars to which I have been invited to present and trial aspects of this book over the past three years. Every single one of those events has allowed me to progress in my thinking. In this category I must single out Vlad Naumescu for inviting me to be part of the Central European Summer School in Budapest in 2015 and allowing staff and students to be subjected to three days of discussion on a cinematic approach to everyday life. I still remember Sergiu raising his hand after my first lecture, asking if it was a serious proposition to spend all this time on such a mundane topic – and managing to enjoy it at the end!

I shouldn't forget of course my privileged interlocutors and *compagnons de route*, Nick Bullock and Dean Hawkes. With Nick I have had endless enjoyable conversations about Henri Lefebvre, while with Dean I carry on having fruitful weekly conversations over lunch in Darwin College.

I am also grateful for Marion Houston's efforts in the last stage of the book in making the text as legible as it now stands, including correcting my French. I would also like to thank Francesca Ford, the Commissioning Editor at Routledge who has patiently accompanied this book together with Trudy Varcianna, the Editorial Assistant. I am also immensely grateful for Joanna Hogg to have authorized the use of stills from *Exhibition* (2013) for the book's cover.

In 2014 I was on sabbatical leave in the south of France, and the village of Fournès provided the perfect setting for my project. Adèle and Jerry Kuehl trusted us with their wonderful house and *les Fournaisans* were most welcoming, Alain Wester in particular, who heroically ran the only shop in the village, our lifeline. My twice daily trip to Alain's formed the basis of *Le journal d'épicerie* – another everyday life project that I have yet to publish – it became the ghostly presence that accompanied this book and comforted me in the study of the *quotidien*.

This book is dedicated to my wife, Fabia, who has accompanied me for over 20 years, patiently and lovingly encouraging and nurturing this project, on an everyday basis.

INTRODUCTION

'Everyday things represent the most overlooked knowledge. These names are vital to your progress. Quotidian things. If they weren't important, we wouldn't use such a gorgeous Latinate word. Say it,' he said.

'Quotidian.'

'An extraordinary word that suggests the depth and reach of the commonplace.'

Underworld *(DeLillo, 2011, p.542)*

Ah, que la vie est quotidienne...

Complainte sur certains ennuis *(Laforgue, 1885, p.79)*

On the eve of sabbatical leave in 2014, I attended a seminar on Georges Perec[1] at which *Les lieux d'une fugue* (Perec, 1978) [Scene of a flight] was screened. Although I had never seen this film, I had long worked on various aspects of Perec's work, in particular his observation techniques in *Espèces d'espaces* (Perec, 1974) that I used in various practise-based moving-image workshops (Penz, 2012). But during the course of this seminar it dawned on me that Perec could become one of the *fils conducteurs* for the book. It was not planned that way and this new course comprehensively derailed an earlier synopsis I had given to Routledge in 2012. However, I stuck with the original title, *Cinematic Aided Design*, but added the subtitle that defines what the book is about, *An Everyday Life Approach to Architecture*. The focus on the everyday was of course the novel element, and it was only later that I recognized that I had long circled around it without quite knowing it. Perhaps this is not surprising, as the everyday is in its very nature invisible, yet ever-present and overlooked; it is in the same league as what prose is to Molière's Monsieur Jourdain:[2] we all practise it without noticing it.

I also became aware with time that working on the everyday was not necessarily all that glamorous or fashionable, and that in the words of Joe Moran I would 'probably need to

2 Introduction

develop a thick skin. Some people may accuse you of trying to rediscover what a certain strain of English pragmatism likes to call "the bleeding obvious"' (Moran, 2008, p.3). But I persisted, encouraged by a resurgence of interest in the everyday: the New York Tribeca 2015 Film Festival showcased movies about everyday life (Reaney, 2015), while it was central to several national pavilions at the 2016 Venice Biennale of Architecture. The British pavilion *Home Economics* focused on the changes in patterns of everyday life, the Taiwanese pavilion was named 'Everyday Architecture Re-made in Taiwan', while the 'Belgian pavilion triumphs once again with a show celebrating architecture of the everyday' (Wainwright, 2016). And in June 2016 the French *Ordre des Architectes* staged a series of national open days under the umbrella of everyday architecture (les architectes ouvrent leurs portes au grand public […] sous le signe de l'architecture du quotidien) (Muuuz Magazine, 2016).

I also realized that I had previously neglected Perec's *le cinématographe*, the film-maker, a part of his oeuvre often unknown and overlooked. The importance of Perec is that he gave me both the cinematic as well as the everyday that are all contained in the opening sequence of *Les lieux d'une fugue* as the voice-over explains the motivations for the film: 'très vite j'ai décidé de me consacrer aux lieux seules de cette fugue…toucher les spectateurs en leur montrant un banc, un arbre, un cartable, un commissariat de police…est devenu pour moi l'essentiel' [very quickly I decided to focus solely on the places related to the running-away episode…to create an emotional bond with the audience by showing a bench, a tree, a satchel, a police station… this became the essential]. The focus of the film is in part on the banality of the everyday environment and everyday life,[3] and it certainly resonated with me. And so the writing of this book has been something of an adventure – or rather I allowed it to be. It started one way and ended up somewhere else. It is only while writing it that the shape of the book revealed itself. I merely became the secretary to my own intellectual bricolage. And it is not just Perec that I rediscovered, but in the process and to my surprise 'I discovered how important to me were, unknowingly, books I had never read, events and persons I did not know had existed' (Ginzburg, 1993, p.34), to which I should add, films that I had never come across before.

But a cinematic approach to everyday life and architecture implies an interdisciplinary approach or, as I would rather think of it, a form of 'indiscipline', experiencing the turbulence or incoherence at the inner and outer boundaries of disciplines whereby a set of collective practices (technical, social, professional, etc.) triggers a moment of breakage or rupture, when the continuity is broken and the practice comes into question (Mitchell, 1995, p.541). The practice that comes into question in this case is architecture, but also my own field which explores the relation between cinema and architecture, a topic that is not clearly defined, its boundaries forever shifting. It remains an amorphous and elusive 'in-discipline'. Cinema and architecture is like a borderless infinite puzzle to which some of us add a piece from time to time, waiting for others to join or to put it another way, 'The amateur's way implies that cinema belongs to all those who have, one way or another, traveled within its system […] and that everyone is authorized to trace one's own itinerary within this topography, adding to the cinema as world and to its knowledge' (Rancière, 2011, p.14).[4] Mitchell adds that his motto has been to 'get by with a little help from his friends'. I too rely on my 'friends' – and my friends are people, books, journals from a wide range of fields – film studies, philosophy, visual culture, psychocinematics, art history, and anthropology, amongst others. They have accompanied me all these years and the numbers grow with time to encompass also other cultures, a form of cultural indisciplinarity.[5] To name but just two, one of my oldest 'friends' is Jacques Tati, who turned everyday observations into a cinematic art form; a more recent acquaintance is Abraham Moles, a constant source of inspiration, with *Micropsychologie et vie quotidienne* [Micropsychology and everyday life] (Moles, 1976) amongst others.

However, I have also realized that no matter how interdisciplinary or indisciplinary my research might be, it remains firmly rooted in the world of architecture. And while I borrow from and venture into other fields, I naturally retreat back to the relative safety of my profession, but always enriched by my indisciplines. For architecture is a profession, not simply an academic discipline, and ultimately all that I produce is first and foremost conscious of architectural education, architectural research and the architecture profession.[6] Thus, from an architect's perspective, one of the key aims of this book is to address the question of post-occupancy, which is a real challenge to architecture. The connection with the cinematic of the everyday may not be at all obvious at first sight and needs some explanation. In turn I will consider the position of the architect followed by that of the film-maker.

We know that architects are good at designing buildings, but we also know that there is little research after a building has been handed over to the client. As a result, architects do not have much information as to how their buildings function after completion. One of the few books on the subject is Brand's *How buildings learn: what happens after they're built* (Brand, 1995). In an RIBA paper on 'Architects and research-based knowledge', Murray Fraser acknowledges that 'There is wide recognition from practitioners of the potential benefits of engaging with research, in particularly Post-Occupancy Evaluation, and its importance to the work of practices. However there is a rift between intention and practice [...] Post-Occupancy Evaluation was identified as a key method to improve design quality and reduce the "performance gap", but there are a number of barriers' (Fraser, 2014, p.3). In other words, most buildings are reduced to mute objects as architects fail to interrogate them in any systematic way.[7]

On the other hand, as soon as the architects move out, having completed a building, the film-makers move in. Figure I.1 illustrates this process. For example, when the new Rolex building (Sanaa architects) in Lausanne was just completed, Wim Wenders started to film – see Plate 1. The resulting movie, *If Buildings Could Talk* (Wenders, 2010), is an interesting case in point as Wenders gave the building a voice, it was no longer silent.[8]

So over the last 120 years, film-makers have archived, expressed, characterized, interpreted and portrayed hundreds of thousands of buildings. Folded away and preserved in celluloid film

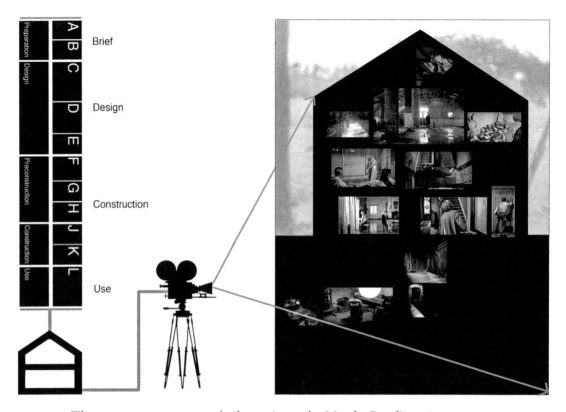

FIGURE I.1 Film as post-occupancy study (house image by Martha Rawlinson)

is a comprehensive encyclopaedia of architectural spaces and building elements and how to use them; doors and windows were opened and closed, stairs were descended, corridors were strolled along, lobbies were entered, walls were bumped into, cellars were visited, attics were inhabited, bedrooms were slept in etc.… the list is far too long to enumerate. And not only were all those spaces lived in, entered and exited but also lit, ventilated, heated, cooled, painted and decorated. Kitchens came in many different colours, shapes and sizes. Meals were cooked, people made love, sofas were sat on, baths were run and showers taken. Films have exposed precious everyday gestures and large fragments of our everyday life. It constitutes an extraordinary archive of lived and practised spaces, a formidable reservoir of post-occupancy studies. In other words, films constitute the most comprehensive lived-in building data in existence – a largely ignored and untapped resource that can be mined in many different ways, and this constitutes the central hypothesis of the book. I have already had the opportunity to exploit this remarkable archive as part of an AHRC research project on Battersea, where through a process of 'cinematic urban archaeology', we excavated the successive cinematic layers of a part of the urban fabric hovering invisibly over Battersea. It allowed us to trace the evolution of the fabric of the city across the twentieth century as well as understanding the social changes that took place at the time (Penz et al., 2017).

To Perec, I added Henri Lefebvre, *l'incontournable* in all matters of the *quotidien*, all the more so as I followed his seminars in 1971 (see Chapter 1). Lefebvre and Perec are spearheading **PART 1** 'An everyday life approach to architecture', consisting of a single chapter, **Chapter 1**, 'The case for everydayness', which is the foundation of this book. Perec is most relevant to architects, given his focus on everyday spaces, while Lefebvre provides us with infinite and lyrical variations on everyday life, a source of constant inspiration. The second part of this chapter deals with a historical perspective on how the everyday was re-interpreted in the US with *Learning from Las Vegas* (Venturi et al., 1972) and by Alison and Peter Smithson in England with the As Found movement. The last part of the chapter deals with the contemporary view of the everyday in the world of architecture, its modern interpretation in the UK in particular. It is also the opportunity to discuss the iconic versus the everyday environment as well as distinguish between everyday life and the everyday environment. Overall this chapter briefly traces the evolution of the notion of the everyday as interpreted then and now from the point of view of architecture. It sets the scene for an exploration of everyday life and architecture through film, which is the subject of the following chapters.

Following **PART 1**, the book is in three parts. **PART 2** elicits the mechanisms by which we can grasp everyday life through cinema. It is divided into five chapters: **Chapter 2** 'Introduction to everydayness and cinema' makes the link with Lefebvre's writing on film and opens the discussion on the link between everyday life and realism, for the two notions are inextricably linked. **Chapter 3** 'The value of fiction and the role of disruptions' is in praise of fiction films, which allow us to grasp a more approachable lived reality, providing an accelerated education in complex situations. The second part of Chapter 3 uncovers the mechanisms by which the everyday life 'baseline' is the necessary fertile ground from which drama will erupt. **Chapter 4** 'Georges Perec and Chantal Akerman' first examines Perec's *le cinématographe* of the everyday with a case study of *L'homme qui dort* (1973), followed by an account of Georges Perec and Chantal Akerman's parallel lives with *Jeanne Dielman* (Akerman, 1974) providing the backdrop for this case study. **Chapter 5** 'Rhythmanalysis' considers Lefebvre's last book, *Rhythmanalysis*, and adapts his way of understanding time and space through the cyclical and linear rhythms of everyday life to film by principally analysing Joanna Hogg's *Exhibition* (2013), a film that takes place in a modernist house. It is here that there is an opportunity to ponder on the relationship between modernism and everyday life. **Chapter 6** 'Cinematic typologies of the everyday' reflects on the possibility to observe and classify cinematic activities of everyday life with a view to creating typologies of inhabited, lived-in and practised architectural forms. However, such typologies could hardly be organized according to built form – as everyday life cannot be systematized in relation to building shapes alone. We have therefore to explore categories and types according to activities, functions, circadian cycles, rhythms, and many other variables.

6 Introduction

PART 3 'An architectonic of cinema' is concerned with key building elements that pertain to architecture – windows, doors, walls, stairs – showing how their many functions are cinematically practised and revealed – throwing new light on building elements that are often taken for granted. It consists of five chapters: **Chapter 7** is the introduction to the whole architectonic of cinema concept, pointing first to Jeanne Dielman's kitchen scenes as having striking similarities with Neufert's Architects' data of prototypical kitchen layouts – thus constituting a textbook 'cinematic kitchen use of everydayness', if only such a thing existed. This introduces the idea of a cinematic encyclopaedia of architectural elements that parallels Rem Koolhaas's *Elements of Architecture* (Koolhaas et al., 2014), the latest offering in a long line of architectural standardization efforts. **Chapter 8** 'Windows' explores cinematic windows as communication, windows for dreaming, windows that separate or windows that unite, windows that interrogate, windows that hide, and many more that challenge or complement the humble everyday window. Windows are not just to let light in and prevent heat from escaping or a means of ventilation, there are a myriad of functions that often go unnoticed but that cinema reveals. **Chapter 9** 'Doors' makes the point that very often a door in a film is associated with a cut, implying and inviting a movement, unlike windows, which are associated with the gaze. Doors are not only an instrument of passage, they also reveal, and can be a contested space or a symbol of rejection while also signalling hope, protection and much more. The door is an active architectonic element imbued with affect, part of architecture as experience. **Chapter 10** 'Stairs' reviews the typology of stairs as presented by architectural historians of building technology but re-interpreted by film-makers such as Hitchcock, Godard and others. In particular it is found that the built-in elements of danger associated with stairs, abundantly documented in architectural treatises, has been more than adequately reflected in film. So far the chapters in Part 3 have concentrated on elements of architecture treated in isolation: windows, doors and stairs. But **Chapter 11** 'Joining the dots' brings the elements of architecture together as whole movie sequences. It is a two-part exploration. The first part considers the rise in scenes portraying lifts, especially in US films, reflecting the potential demise of the staircase as an architectural element. This observation demonstrates how entrances combined with lifts and corridors have become 'shorthand' for a building. The second part is a case study of the flat scene in Godard's *Le Mépris* (1963) that brings together windows, doors and stairs but also walls, corridors, corners, ceilings and floors – effectively 'joining the dots', something that film is particularly good at.

PART 4 'Cinematic aided design' is a single chapter that also acts as the conclusion and therefore closes the loop of Figure I.1. It essentially points to potential avenues for architects to exploit. Film-makers have 'taken' from architecture; it is time for architects to get something back from this process. Cinema has, mostly unwittingly, provided a formidable reservoir of post-occupancy studies. Closing the loop implies a process of restitution from film to architecture. However, this is not a book that provides recipes but rather a rationale for what could be achieved. *Cinematic Aided Design*, being a play of words on *Computer Aided Design* (CAD), implies that we need this injection of cinematic intelligence to enrich the design process. The final section of Part 4 explores the concepts of *situations* and *atmospheres*, opening new insights in relation to the everyday. Regarding the first point, I posit that film provides us with a formidable array of interpretive human situations, and that it exposes hidden strata of everyday life that would otherwise be inaccessible to us. Film helps us to attain something like fragments or moments of atmospheres, pertaining to everyday life situations. But while there are many overlaps between a cinematic atmosphere and an architectural atmosphere, there are no easy ways to transfer from one to the other. This is a complex 'model', which opens potential new avenues yet to be investigated, and one that pertains to the world of cinematic-assisted imagination.

Notes

1   The seminar was entitled *Georges Perec's Scene of a Flight: Mnemotechnics on Screen* and the speaker was Dr Mark Goodall (University of Bradford) to whom I am grateful for having unwittingly fostered this change of direction.
2   Monsieur Jourdain is the main character in Molière's *Le Bourgeois gentilhomme* (1670). He is rich, middle class and idle, and in his attempt to be accepted as an aristocrat he takes some philosophy lessons on language. To his delight, he learns that he has been speaking prose all his life without knowing it: *'Par ma foi ! il y a plus de quarante ans que je dis de la prose sans que j'en susse rien, et je vous suis le plus obligé du monde de m'avoir appris cela'*.
3   *Les Lieux d'une Fugue* (1978) is originally a text that Perec wrote in 1965 and which was adapted for the screen and shot in 1976 and first aired on television in 1978. Perec published the text for the first time in 1976. The story is autobiographical and deceptively simple: 'C'était le 11 mai 1947. Il avait 11 ans et 2 mois. Il venait de s'enfuir de chez lui, 18 rue de l 'Assomption, 16ème arrondissement'. In 1945, a young Perec ran away from the family home – uncle and ant – and played truand for a day and part of a night. He was later found by a man while attempting to sleep on a bench on the Champ Elysées, taken to a police station, and later collected by his uncle. However, Perec only remembered, and subsequently wrote that story some 20 years later, in 1965, while revisiting a key place of the 'fugue', 'le marché aux timbres', on the Champ Elysées. Indeed Perec used to collect stamps as a child and in the running away episode, he had hoped to sell some of his collection to make some pocket money.
4   My translation from the French 'La politique de l'amateur affirme que le cinéma appartient à tous ceux qui ont, d'une manière ou d'une autre, voyagé à l'intérieur du système d'écarts que son nom dispose et que chacun peut s'autoriser à tracer, entre tel ou tel point de cette topographie, un itinéraire singulier qui ajoute au cinéma comme monde et à sa connaissance' (Rancière, 2011, p.14).
5   I am referring here to my AHRC research project (2017–2020) entitled *A Cinematic Musée Imaginaire of Spatial Cultural Differences* – that endeavours to reveal and elicit spatial cultural differences, through the film medium, across different cultures, China/Japan v. Europe /US in particular.
6   I am also hoping that other disciplines, for example film studies and cultural studies, would also benefit from my explorations, thus making a contribution to a 'deep' interdisciplinary approach as opposed to a 'shallow' one.
7   However, this is gradually changing as the RIBA Plan of Work 2013 now incorporates Post-Occupancy Evaluation: 'Post-Occupancy Evaluation is not only an explicit part of the new Stage 7 (along with a review of project performance, project outcome and research and development) but the

review of the findings from previous projects is included in Stage 0, with the intention of closing the feedback loop, and binding research more tightly into project processes' (Fraser, 2014, p.7).

8   My transcript from a lecture that Wenders gave at the Venice Biennale in 2010: '[...] so I spent days and days in the building [...] observing the people who were using the buildings [...] I thought I understood the dialogue between the building and its users – and I understood its primary function which is to make people meet – an extraordinary place of communication – so I wrote the toughest dialogue I ever wrote for my movies – I wrote a monologue – and it was a great relief when I heard this beautiful voice and I thought Hei! the building is talking'.

References

Brand, S. (1995) *How buildings learn: what happens after they're built.* New York: Penguin.

DeLillo, D. (2011) *Underworld.* London: Picador.

Fraser, M. (2014) Architects and research-based knowledge: a literature review. *Royal Institute of British Architects.*

Ginzburg, C. (1993) Microhistory: two or three things that I know about it. *Critical Inquiry.* 20 (1), 10–35.

Koolhaas, R. et al. (2014) *Elements of architecture.* Venice: Marsilio Editori Spa.

Laforgue, J. (1885) *Les complaintes.* Paris: Léon Vanier.

Mitchell, W. J. T. (1995) Interdisciplinarity and Visual Culture. *The Art Bulletin.* 77 (4), 540–544.

Moles, A. (1976) *Micropsychologie et vie quotidienne.* Paris: Editions Denoël / Gonthier.

Moran, J. (2008) *Queuing for beginners: the story of daily life from breakfast to bedtime.* London: Profile Books.

Muuuz Magazine (2016) *Les architectes ouvrent leurs portes : l'architecture du quotidien* [online]. Available from: http://www.archidesignclub.com/magazine/actualites/agenda/47739-les-architectes-ouvrent-leurs-portes-l-architecture-du-quotidien.html (Accessed 15 June 2016).

Penz, F. (2012) Towards an urban narrative layers approach to decipher the language of city films. *Comparative Literature and Culture.* 14 (3) [online]. Available from: http://docs.lib.purdue.edu/clcweb/vol14/iss3/7/ (Accessed 28 April 2016).

Penz, F. et al. (2017) 'Cinematic Urban Archaeology: the Battersea case', in François Penz and Richard Koeck (eds) *Cinematic Urban Geographies.* New York: Palgrave Macmillan.

Perec, G. (1974) *Espèces d'espaces.* Espace critique. Paris: Galilée.

Rancière, J. (2011) *Les écarts du cinéma.* La Fabrique éditions.

Reaney, P. (2015) *Tribeca Film Festival showcases movies about 'everyday life'. | Reuters* [online]. Available from: http://uk.reuters.com/article/uk-film-tribeca-idUKKBN0M001720150304 (Accessed 23 December 2016).

Venturi, R. et al. (1972) *Learning from Las Vegas.* Cambridge, Mass.: MIT Press.

Wainwright, O. (2016) Venice architecture biennale pavilions – a souped-up pre-school playground. *The Guardian.* 30 May. [online]. Available from: https://www.theguardian.com/artanddesign/2016/may/30/venice-architecture-biennale-2016-national-pavilions-review (Accessed 23 December 2016).

PART 1

An everyday life approach to architecture

1

THE CASE FOR EVERYDAYNESS

Il y a un siècle, qui aurait cru possible d'étudier avec le plus grand sérieux scientifique les balbutiements de l'enfant ou les rougeurs de l'adolescence ? Ou la forme des maisons ? Dans la mesure où la science de l'homme existe, elle trouve sa matière dans le banal, dans le quotidien. Et c'est elle, la connaissance, qui a frayé la voie à notre conscience. [Who would have thought it possible a century ago that the first hesitant words of infants or the blushes of adolescents – or the shape of houses – would become the objects of serious scientific study? In so far as the science of man exists, it finds its material in the banal, in the everyday. And it is the science of man – knowledge – which has blazed the trail for our consciousness.]

(Lefebvre, 1958, p.146)[1]

This first section is essentially concerned with providing an overview of the current position on the everyday that pertains to the world of architecture. However, in doing so I am not attempting to redefine what the everyday is. Rather, I am preparing the ground for what is, I believe, a new approach, that is to study the everyday through the medium of film with a view to provide not only architects, planners, designers, practitioners, but also politicians and decision-makers with a new awareness of the everyday. I suggest concentrating on how spaces are being used and practised by cinema, so the type of everydayness I am interested in is the daily use of our everyday spaces – the streets we use every day, the transport we take routinely to go to work, the workplaces we inhabit – but with an emphasis on the home, houses and dwellings in general. All of those spaces are used, to paraphrase Walter Benjamin, in a state of distraction (Benjamin, 2007, p.239), and therefore need to be constantly reassessed. I will therefore start by considering the everyday through my own lens, starting by 'clearing the ground', not through a comprehensive review of the field but by highlighting what is here relevant for my hypothesis, a necessary step towards establishing the conceptual basis for this book.

12 An everyday life approach to architecture

It would be difficult not to start with Henri Lefebvre, who devoted three large volumes to the study of the everyday, spanning over 30 years of his life: *Critique de la vie quotidienne* (1947, 1961 and 1981). In his 1961 second edition – *Critique de la vie quotidienne – Fondements d'une sociologie de la quotidienneté* [Foundations for a Sociology of the Everyday], he states his objective as 'The object of our study is everyday life, with the idea, or rather the project (the programme), of transforming it' (Lefebvre, 2014, p.296). Paradoxically, while attempting to transform it, Lefebvre found it challenging to define precisely what everyday life is. Indeed a lot of the writing in the three volumes of *Critique de la vie quotidienne* (hereafter I will abbreviate the title to *Critique*) is devoted to successive refinement of the definition: 'How can everyday life be defined? It surrounds us, it besieges us, on all sides and from all directions' (Lefebvre, 2014, p.335), further acknowledging the difficulty of the project.

> In one sense there is nothing more simple and more obvious than everyday life. How do people live? The question may be difficult to answer, but that does not make it any the less clear. In another sense, nothing could be more superficial: it is banality, triviality, *repetitiveness*. And in yet another sense nothing could be more profound. It is existence and the 'lived', revealed as they are before speculative thought has transcribed them: what must be changed and what is the hardest of all to change.
>
> *(Lefebvre, 2014, p.341)*

As a result, many of his readers have acknowledged that 'Lefebvre's concept of everyday life is elusive, due in part to his intensely dialectical approach and his refusal of any static categorization' (Berke and Harris, 1997, p.13). Poignantly Lefebvre states that 'we are moving closer to a detailed and precise definition of everyday life' (Lefebvre, 2014, p.355), but in the last page of the last volume, *The Epilogue*, he states 'to finish this conclusion, which in no sense is definitive or conclusive' (Lefebvre, 2014, p.842), thus inferring that the project was indeed open ended. Lefebvre also clearly rejected the idea of establishing a 'closed system'.[2] I therefore construe *Critique* as an 'open system' from which we can borrow, pursue, expand and interpret. And by 'open system' I mean that there is such a richness of thinking in *Critique* that it is open to multiple interpretation. *Critique* operates like a 'fractal text': whenever one delves deeper into Lefebvre's writing, the same problems and complexity keep appearing, but reformulated in different ways.[3]

Particularly interesting in Lefebvre's project is the idea that the everyday has clear potential for creative inspiration: 'it is in everyday life and starting from everyday life that genuine creations are achieved', which stresses the potential for 'works of creativity' (Lefebvre, 2014, p.338). There is also a clear sense of optimism that indeed the everyday can contribute to changes: 'Vague images of the future and man's prospects are inadequate. These images allow for too many more-or-less technocratic or humanist interpretations. If we are to know and to judge, we must start with a precise criterion and a centre of reference: the everyday' (Lefebvre,

2014, p.340). I will take this as one of my starting points, that is to say that the everyday concept can be an agent of change and a work of creativity. *Critique de la vie quotidienne* accompanies this project on many different levels and throughout this book.

Other major influences pertaining to the elaboration of the concept of the everyday have to be acknowledged, as succinctly summarized by Sheringham:[4]

> Between 1960 and 1980 the evolving ideas of Lefebvre, Barthes, Perec, and Certeau fed into and drew on each of the others [...] and made this a vital period in the emergence of the everyday as a paradigm. But one of the features that does make them different from one another (whilst enhancing the collective power of their contributions) is that these authors emerged from different intellectual traditions [...]. In the broadest of terms, Lefebvre can be associated with humanist Marxism, Barthes with Structuralism and its evolution into post-structuralism and post-modernism, Certeau with history, anthropology, and psychoanalysis, and Perec with the literary experimentalism of the Oulipo group, inaugurated by Raymond Queneau.
>
> *(Sheringham, 2006, p.9)*

But aside from Lefebvre, the other towering figure of the everyday who is very prominent in this book is Georges Perec.

Lefebvre and Perec

If Lefebvre is *l'incontournable* who provides an infinite matrix of quotidian inspirations to which I will return time and time again, it is Perec who supplied me with *le fil conducteur* and the motivation for this book. There is a level of abstraction in Lefebvre that makes his work open to multiple interpretations, while Perec's prose is far more down to earth and yet poetic at the same time. Perec equips us with novel spatial methods of observations of the everyday, that in a later chapter I translate to film analysis. *Espèces d'espaces* [Species of Spaces] (1974) gave me the structure for analyzing 'the species of cinematic spaces'. And if this was not enough, Perec was also a film-maker and the inventor of *l'écriture-cinéma* (Peytard, 1997, pp.33–37). In other words, the difference between Lefebvre and Perec regarding the everyday is that Lefebvre theorizes it while Perec is 'doing it' and demonstrates how it works from the 'inside'.

In *Espèces d'espaces, le quotidien* is only mentioned three times in 183 pages [French edition] although it is completely central to the book as expressed by Perec in his very first words in the *prière d'insérer*:[5]

> The space of our life is neither continuous, nor infinite, neither homogeneous, nor isotropic. But do we really know where it shatters, where it curves, and where it assembles

itself? We feel a confused sensation of cracks, hiatus, points of friction, sometimes we have the vague impression that it is getting jammed somewhere, or that it is bursting, or colliding. We rarely try to know more about it and more often than not go from one place to another, from one space to another without trying to measure, to grasp, to consider these gaps in space. The issue is not to invent space, and even less to re-invent it (too many well-meaning people are responsible for thinking about our environment…), but to interrogate it, or to just read it; because what we call everydayness is not evidence but opacity: a form of blindness, a mode of anaesthesia. It's from those basic remarks that this book has developed, a diary of a user of space.[6]

(Perec, 1974)

Perec's writing is particularly attractive and relevant for architects, as it is about space and everyday spaces and how they are lived in and practised. Perec commits to the everyday, inhabits it, breathes it and adheres to it. The everyday is Perec's *matière brut*, his primary writing material, which figures at the very top of his list of preoccupations: 'La première de ces interrogations peut être qualifiée de 'sociologique': comme de regarder le quotidien; elle est au départ de textes comme *Les Choses, Espèces d'espaces, Tentative de description de quelques lieux parisiens*' [the first of these questions could be construed as 'sociological': as when observing the quotidian, it is the starting point for texts such as *Les Choses, Espèces d'espaces, Tentative de description de quelques lieux parisiens*] (Perec, 2003, p.10). Perec also alludes to the creation of new 'disciplines', *l'infra-ordinaire* and *l'endotique*.[7] He hints at a literary enterprise associated with an anthropology of proximity and a sociology of the everyday. Schilling rightly remarks that writing on the quotidian in the French context of the 1960s and 1970s is hardly innocent, and that with his new brand of 'sociologie de la quotidienneté' Perec was hinting at much more than he expressed and much less than he could have, given the abundance of literature on the topic of the everyday, in particular from Lefebvre (Schilling, 2006, p.19).

But it would be pointless to put Lefebvre and Perec in opposition, as they were not competing with each other in the way that, for example, Debord and Lefebvre did at some point.[8] Perec was not an academic and none of his work contains any traditional references or bibliographies – if anything, he was quite capable of inventing them, mixing the real with the imaginary, as if 'covering his tracks'. Yet his work has an extraordinary internal rigour that he drew from his association with the *L'OuLiPo*[9] group and working with self-imposed constraints [*les contraintes*],[10] a method of working that later appealed to Bernard Tschumi for the Parc de La Villette as he refers to Queneau and Perec for his use of *transformations oulipiennes* (Tschumi, 2004, p.124).

There is an obvious complementarity between Lefebvre and Perec, which is not surprising given the nature of their collaboration and friendship[11] in the 1950s and 1960s (Lefebvre, 2014, p.658). Both collaborated extensively with architects and schools of architecture. From 1968 onwards Lefebvre was very involved with architects and urbanists, from both a theoretical

```
ECOLE POLYTECHNIQUE FEDERALE DE LAUSANNE
DEPARTEMENT D'ARCHITECTURE                          MAI 1971.
FF/pem/8ème semestre.


HENRI   LEFEBVRE : bibliographie
_____


Le nationalisme contre les Nations              e.s.i. 1937
Hitler au pouvoir: bilan de 5 années de fascisme   Bureau d'edition 1938.
en Allemagne

Nietzsche                                        e.s.i. 1939

L'existentialisme                                ed.du Sagittaire 1946

Critique de la vie quotidienne          vol.1    Grasset 1946
                                                 L'Arche 1958
                                        vol.2    L'Arche 1961

Le matérialisme dialectique                      Alcan 1939
                                                 4ème éd. 1959

Marx et la liberté                               Genève 1947

Le marxisme                                      PUF 1948
```

FIGURE 1.1 Extract from the bibliography from Henri Lefebvre's handout (1971)[12]

and a practical point of view. He lectured in numerous schools of architecture in France as well as abroad, in particular at the School of Architecture in Lausanne (Ecole Polytechnique Fédérale de Lausanne) where I was studying. I was fortunate to follow his teaching in 1971, in my first year of architecture, and it is very clear from his bibliography that as students we were expected to familiarize ourselves not only with the first two volumes of *Critique* and his writing on cities, but also with Marxism and Leninism.

We were part of a generation that had been enormously influenced by May 1968, and were by and large politically engaged. It is therefore unsurprising that in his handout Lefebvre acknowledges, in front of the staff, that the school 'was not catering to the preoccupations and needs of the student and that therefore the students should take charge of their own teaching'… quite unthinkable nowadays, but part of the zeitgeist at the time, the spirit of *contestation* was still rife, even in Switzerland (see Figure 1.2 below).

```
IL apparaît de plus en plus, et c'est vrai pour ce département d'architecture,
que les préoccupations des étudiants ne correspondent plus au cadre de l'ensei-
gnement proposé. Les étudiants sont amenés à prendre en main leur enseignement
et à le diriger selon leurs propres préoccupations.
```

FIGURE 1.2 Extract from Henri Lefebvre's handout (1971)

16 An everyday life approach to architecture

He was also invited to judge prestigious architectural competitions and actively participated in urban projects – this has been well documented by Stanek[13] (Stanek, 2011) and need not be elaborated further. However, it is useful to note that Lefebvre gained international prominence essentially through his work on urban studies, with the publication of *Le droit à la ville* in 1968 and later *La production de l'espace* (1974), translated into English[14] in 1996 and 1991 respectively – but the everyday was always present in relation to his writing on the right to the city.[15]

As for Perec, his first contact with the world of architecture dates back to 1971–1972, when Jean Duvignaud launched *Cause Commune* with Paul Virilio, who at the time was the director of L'Ecole Spéciale d'Architecture in Paris (Roche, 2015, p.59). He was also often solicited to be part of *jurys de thèses*, and attended studio crits in schools of architecture (Roche, 2015, p.60) where he also gave conferences and participated in various colloquia.[16] However, he was also quite critical of modern architecture, most notably in his text *l'inhabitable* [the uninhabitable], which reads like an inventory of architectural failures: 'The uninhabitable [...] foul cities. The uninhabitable: a showy architecture of contempt, the mediocre vainglory of towers and buildings, the thousands of rabbit hutches piled on top of another [...] The uninhabitable: the slums, the fake cities' (Perec, 1974, p.176).[17] This has to be put in the context of the rapid housing developments that took place in post-WWII France. Over the years Perec's reputation has grown considerably in schools of architecture[18] and his *Species of Spaces* has been widely adopted as a key text on space, on a par with Bachelard's *La poétique de l'espace* [The Poetics of Space] (Bachelard, 1957).

The everyday and architecture – a historical perspective – from France to the US and the UK

The notion of everydayness has taken a while to reach the architectural shores. However, I have to first mention a curious book, dating from 1924 and entitled *Everyday Architecture*, that I believe to be the very first book containing those two words in the title. Its author, Manning Robertson, an architect,[19] had of course no inkling of the Lefebvre scholarship to come, instead, he noted that:

> If the average man were asked for his views on everyday architecture, he would probably reply, once his astonishment had subsided, that there is no such thing; and he would be perfectly right, in the sense that architecture is commonly associated only with cathedrals, town halls, monuments and such technicalities as dog-tooth mouldings and Corinthian capitals.
>
> *(Robertson, 1924, p.19)*[20]

It is difficult to blame the architecture profession, given the elusiveness of a subject that by its very nature is so hard to pin down and define. The everyday is a branch of cultural studies, philosophy and sociology, and its intangibility is by definition at odds with material culture, of which the world of architecture is part. How do we focus on what escapes us? Maurice Blanchot sums up this conundrum admirably:

> The Everyday is the hardest thing to uncover [...] The everyday is human. The earth, the sea, forest, light, night, do not represent everydayness, which belongs first of all to the dense presence of great urban centers. We need these admirable deserts that are the world's cities for the experience of the everyday to begin to overtake us.
>
> *(Blanchot and Hanson, 1987, p.12)*

The everyday is associated with the built environment and all human activities, which makes it all the more poignant and necessary for the design professions to get a grasp on this notion... but how?

I would venture that the moment when the key protagonists of the everyday and the world of architecture finally came together in an 'official platform', was in 1981, on the occasion of *Construire pour Habiter* [Building homes], an exhibition in Paris and a publication that celebrated the tenth anniversary of the French *Plan Construction*. This was at the tail-end of a period in France of intense reflection on housing and urban issues, a major preoccupation of the *Trente Glorieuses* (1946–1975) and a fertile ground for *Le quotidien* and its association with dwellings: 'how profound is everything involving the house, the "home" and domesticity, and thus everyday life' (Lefebvre, 2014, p.516). Paul Delouvrier, in his introduction to the catalogue, states that '250 millions [francs] have been devoted to research in all aspects of the field of housing, including the "sociological": a key fact and one of the original characteristics of the Plan Construction' (Allain-Dupré Fabry and Lavalou, 1981).[21] And if we consult the list of contributors to *Construire pour Habiter*, we find an astonishing line-up of all the key players of the everyday; Lefebvre, Perec, de Certeau, Luce Giard,[22] Michel Maffesoli[23] as well as others, matched by key architects of the time, amongst whom were Paul Chemetov, Paul Virilio and Bernard Huet. *Construire pour Habiter*'s theme was not the everyday, although it was very present,[24] and the main initiators of the thinking regarding the *quotidien* had been conveyed to partake in a debate about the future of housing. While Perec wrote a characteristically poetic text entitled 'A few usages of the verb to inhabit' [*De quelques emplois du verbe habiter*] (Allain-Dupré Fabry and Lavalou, 1981, p.2), Lefebvre's short text 'To inhabit: the awakening of architectural thinking' [*Habiter : L'éveil et le réveil de la pensée architecturale*] starts by 'Talking to architects...' [*Parlant avec des architectes...*] (Allain-Dupré Fabry and Lavalou, 1981, p.18) and pursues a line of thinking about the conception of architectural and urban projects that clearly shows that he was well versed in conversing with architects.

The notion of the everyday in the US

While the notion of the everyday had started to enter architectural discourse in France and other francophone countries in the 1960s, 1970s and 1980s, this was not the case for Anglo-Saxon countries, due to a lack of English translations.[25] *Critique de la vie quotidienne – introduction* [1947] was first translated in 1991, 44 years later; *Critique de la vie quotidienne – Fondements d'une sociologie de la quotidienneté* [1961] was only translated 41 years later in 2002 – while the third volume published in French in 1981 became available in English in 2005. Curiously *La vie quotidienne dans le monde moderne* (1968) was available in English from 1971.[26] As a result, the concern for the everyday in American architectural circles in the 1960s took a different turn.[27]

However, one of the best documented attempts by architects to engage with the everyday in the US must be Venturi, Scott Brown and Izenour's work, *Learning from Las Vegas* (Venturi et al., 1972). It is a work of great relevance to the everyday but also more broadly, within our context, is important for its methodological approach and its use of film as a mode of observation.[28] The systematic use of moving images for the analysis and representation of the city and urban form, by means of the so-called 'deadpan' method[29] – where a camera is mounted on the bonnet of a car – has been carefully documented by Stierli (Stierli, 2013, pp.149–189).

Learning from Las Vegas was followed in 1976 by *Signs of Life, Symbols in the American City*, an exhibition of everyday American building forms at the Smithsonian Institution. According to Deborah Fausch, *Signs of Life* was not a success and was 'of all their work, perhaps the least well understood' (Berke and Harris, 1997, p.78). In her attempt to understand the negative reactions to the exhibition, Fausch hypothesizes that Venturi and Scott Brown may have struggled to arrive at an intellectual and theoretical stance for thinking about the everyday that has ultimately detracted from their creation of an architecture of the everyday (Berke and Harris, 1997, p.98). Venturi had been interested in the everyday for some time, stating that '[...] it is perhaps from the everyday landscape, vulgar and disdained, that we can draw the complex and contradictory order that is valid and vital for our architecture as an urbanistic whole', adding the much-quoted '...is not Main Street almost all right?' [from *Complexity and Contradiction in Architecture* (1966)].[30]

In that respect, Lefebvre is also particularly lyrical when considering the street, and would have unwittingly given credence to Venturi's study of the Las Vegas strip '...the street represents the everyday in our social life [...] Like the everyday, the street is constantly changing and always repeats itself [...] Almost an absolute spectacle, but not completely, it is an open book, or rather a newspaper: it has news, banalities, surprises, advertisements [...] The street confronts us with a social text which is generally good, dense and legible. [...] Through the interplay of objects offered and refused, the street becomes a place of dreams and imagination' (Lefebvre, 2014, pp.310–312). For Lefebvre, 'main street is definitely ok'!

In stating that 'Architects can no longer afford to be intimidated by the puritanically moral language of orthodox Modern architecture [...] I am for messy vitality over obvious unity' [from

Complexity and Contradiction in Architecture (1966)], Venturi rejected the modernist ideal in favour of the common, the ordinary and the everyday, a move that was seen as deeply controversial. A polemic ensued, in particular with Frampton: 'The dilemma for architects in the post-war period was that the forms that industrial society had arrived at on its own did not correspond to architects' views of how the new society ought to look and function' (Berke and Harris, 1997, p.89). Clearly Frampton thought architects had an obligation to propose something better. An architecture based on everydayness was therefore unacceptable to many and had its limitations for some, as summed up by Mcleod: 'Although the radical aesthetic programs of the Independent Group in the 1950s and of Robert Venturi and Denise Scott Brown in the 1960s and '70s come closer to Lefebvre's vision of "the extraordinary in the ordinary," their critique rarely extended beyond the aesthetic sphere' (Berke and Harris, 1997, p.28).

Venturi, Scott Brown and Izenour's thesis was based on an analysis of everyday urban forms that was in part inspired by the rise of photography and was concerned with the ordinary and the banal, in particular through the work of Ed Ruscha.[31] There were also some acknowledged influences from Alison and Peter Smithson[32] – see the discussion in the next section. However, my understanding is that there was no overlap at the time with the growing studies in *Le quotidien* taking place in France, partly because of the slowness at translating Lefebvre's work into English, as mentioned above.

The fact that on both sides of the Atlantic in the 1960s and 1970s there was a growing interest in the everyday without much overlap between the two can probably be attributed to some form of zeitgeist. Of course there were marked differences between the two approaches. Venturi and Scott Brown were essentially inspired by the transformations of the urban American landscape and promoted their ideas through publications and public exhibitions, while in France the interest in the everyday was essentially philosophical, political and theoretical. The French movement was attempting to grasp the immateriality of everyday life with a view to transforming it, while the American movement was steeped in the ordinary materiality of the urban environment as a source of inspiration. Bringing together the *quotidien* and 'pop art' might seem unusual, but there are clearly important points of contact relevant to this study, particularly in relation to architecture.

The notion of the everyday in the UK

The everyday in the UK, or rather in England, and its relevance to architecture, took yet another turn. 'Pop art' was not a major influence, but photography played a key role, especially Nigel Henderson's photographs of London's East End.[33]

These were a major influence on Alison and Peter Smithson, who used Henderson's work to present their views at the ninth CIAM, highlighting the connections between house–street–district–city, an important contribution to the formation of Team 10. There is no need to dwell on this well-documented history, but I would like to single out one book, *As Found: The Discovery of the Ordinary*, edited by Lichtenstein and Schregenberger (2001), as it brings together previously unconnected strands under the umbrella of the As Found concept, connecting the ordinary with architecture, film and other art forms in England in the 1950s and 1960s. In particular they argue that:

> The designation *As Found* probably originated with the architects Alison and Peter Smithson. They only began to write about it, as far as we know, in 1990, but they had used it as a concept much earlier. It played a big role in a group of young and close-knit artists and architects, a system of axes in which all of the members were equal: the Smithsons, the artist Eduardo Paolozzi, the photographer Nigel Henderson and the journalist Reyner Banham.
>
> *(Lichtenstein and Schregenberger, 2001, p.8)*

Interestingly, the 'discovery of the ordinary' is attributed to architects – and there is no explicit connection to Lefebvre.[34] And it is well worth considering here the Smithsons' short statement about the ordinary and the banal:

> The ordinary and banal: The objective of architecture is the works of art that are lived in. The city is the largest and at present the worst of such works of art. Functionalism [to speak roughly of the heroic period of modern architecture] was a new dream exploiting a new source of geometric and organizational procedures, not a change of objective. [...] That the architecture of the next step is in pursuit of the ordinary and the banal does not mean that it has lost sight of its objective. Ordinariness and banality are the art source for the new situation. The kinds of repetition and control that are now offered to building by industry can be edged towards a kind of dreaming neutrality – an urban equivalent of the Alsace of *Jules and Jim*.
>
> *(Lichtenstein and Schregenberger, 2001, p.141)*

As if pre-empting the sort of criticism Frampton would later level at Venturi et al., the Smithsons make the case for finding inspiration in the ordinary and the banal but without losing sight of their objective: 'a kind of dreaming neutrality – an urban equivalent of the Alsace of *Jules and Jim*'. The reference to Truffaut's film implies, I think, that a celebrated film of the French New Wave, shot amidst very ordinary architectural settings, achieved groundbreaking status, partly thanks to the contrasting banality of the Alsatian environment with the modernism of the cinematography, the dialogues, the use of found footage etc. The implication is that new forms of urban architecture can be invented out of banal settings.

Another characteristic of As Found as a method of working is that it relies on the second glance. As Found is an approach that first neutralizes and then starts anew. Anything that is conventionally considered unfitting, banal or not worthy of mention can now be seen as entirely different: as fitting, fascinating and substantial [...] As Found has to do with attentiveness, with concern for that which exists, with a passion for the task of making something from something. It is a technique of reaction [...] Only the perception of reality launches the activities of designing or producing.

(Lichtenstein and Schregenberger, 2001, p.10)

As an English movement it is characteristically understated, there are no grand gestures or philosophical manifesto, yet it is broad and far-reaching and rooted in various overlapping artistic practices.

Crucially within our context is the link between the As Found movement and cinema. First 'Free Cinema' emerged, closely followed and associated with the so-called Kitchen Sink movement. Free Cinema was a successor to the British Documentary Movement and an important precursor to the British New Wave (Kuhn and Westwell, 2012). The Free Cinema group was founded in 1956 and comprised Lindsay Anderson, Karel Reisz, Tony Richardson and Lorenza Mazzetti. Central to their manifesto was 'a belief in freedom, in the importance of people and the significance of the everyday' (Lichtenstein and Schregenberger, 2001, p.257). The Free Cinema group came together in February 1956, when three of their films were screened at the National Film Theatre in London: Anderson's *O Dreamland* (1953), Karel Reisz and Richardson's *Momma Don't Allow* (1956) and Mazzetti's *Together* (1956). Mazzetti's film featured Eduardo Paolozzi as one of the two deaf-mute dockworkers navigating London's East End that had been comprehensively documented by Nigel Henderson. Paolozzi was therefore a crucial link between the Free Cinema group and the Smithsons. The Free Cinema movement has often been construed as Britain's equivalent of the French New Wave – but much more political:

There were in fact hardly any everyday characters in British cinema. In British cinema realistic working-class figures like those of the 60s were something totally new. Before they had to be either comic or criminal. I think Free Cinema was more politicized in this sense than the Nouvelle Vague in France.

(Lichtenstein and Schregenberger, 2001, p.232)

Later in the 1960s the ideals of the Free Cinema group became part of the Kitchen Sink movement, as most of its members – Anderson, Reisz and Richardson – became associated with the new trend.[35]

The Kitchen Sink movement was concerned with social and societal problems in a way that the French New Wave was not. There was a strong focus on realism and the characters usually came from the working classes with storylines that treated of ordinary subjects and everyday events and drama such as abortions, slum clearance, the rise of youth violence etc. But there were other features in common with the French New Wave, as they shared several characteristic features of 'auteur cinema' including radically new methodology, afforded by new equipment and especially shooting on location as opposed to in the studio. Lightweight cameras and improved film stock allowed for much smaller and more mobile film crews (Lichtenstein and Schregenberger, 2001, pp.238–240). By associating architecture and cinema around the concern for the everyday and its creative potential, the As Found movement presents a unique characteristic that marks it out from the study of the everyday in France and the US.

The everyday and architecture – a contemporary view

> Between the houses of childhood and death, between those of play and work, stands the house of everyday life, which architects have called many things – residence, habitation, dwelling, etc. – as if life could develop in one place only.
>
> *(Rossi, 2010, p.55)*

As mentioned in the previous section, when I followed Lefebvre's seminars in 1971, the study of the everyday implied an attempt to change life, and it was a politically motivated ambition. In the decades that followed, Lefebvre's ideas on the everyday found favour mainly in Cultural Studies, while his work on the city – *Le droit à la ville* (Lefebvre, 2009) and *La production de l'espace* (Lefebvre, 1986) – became popular in urban studies circles. But what about the world of architecture post-Lefebvre, in the 1990s and beyond? By the mid-1990s, the big waves of the *quotidien* of the 1960s and 1970s had long subsided and the lapping was barely audible – in part, as argued by Upton, because 'For an enterprise that exalts the concrete, the study of everyday life is remarkably vague about its object [...] [...] The same vagueness about the nature of everyday life plagues architecture' (Upton, 2002, p.707). Indeed the everyday is eminently suited as a branch of philosophy, given its intangibility, but is clearly at odds with material culture. However, in the late 1990s and early 2000s there was a flurry of excitement in the shape of a couple of edited books (Berke and Harris, 1997; Read, 2000), special issues of *Architectural Design* (*AD*) (Wigglesworth and Till, 1998) and *Daidalos* (Confurius, 2000).

Yet it is clear to me that the everyday was not theorized any more; it is as if architects stumbled into it by trying to make sense of it. The spark had gone, partly because housing wasn't so much on the agenda as it was in the 1960s and 1970s, and we know from Lefebvre that the everyday is best expressed and understood in the domestic environment that so profoundly harbours and nurtures everyday life. The urgency had somewhat waned. And the study of everyday life, translated to architectural speak, concentrated on the 'everyday environment'. It became a different sort of preoccupation, perfectly expressed in Frank-Bertholt Raith's article 'Everyday architecture – in what style should we build?' (Raith, 2000, p.7) and in which he rightly goes on to state that 'instead of asking about the relationship of architectural form to the everyday, we should enquire as to its role in everyday life. But how much do architects know about the everyday qualities of their buildings?' Raith asks all the right questions here regarding what might constitute an everyday architecture and how it might influence everyday life. At the same time he hints that after all, architects don't know much about how their buildings are used (due to the lack of post-occupancy studies, a point I already discussed in the introduction), making it nearly impossible to assess the role of the built environment on everyday life. It is precisely the challenge that film will be able to answer, as we will see in the next chapter.

Ben Highmore in the same journal asks germane questions – but steeped in an understanding of the everyday in cultural studies, his own field: 'the everyday might also require dwelling on as well as dwelling in. It might require a form of attention that can register the unremarkable, make noticeable the unnoticed' (Highmore, 2000, p.38), before reflecting that an

> architectural practice that is capable of responding to this intellectual tradition might not be one that merely attempts to fulfill the demands of the buildings' inhabitants, but one that can interrupt the logic that renders the everyday void. It might be a practice that allows the sensual and stubborn passions of the daily to be directed purposefully against the ideology of 'tradition'. A house of material memory opposed to the constructed memory of nation, for instance. It might be a practice that works to disrupt the commodification of time and space, or else makes such commodification unliveable. What would an architecture be like that would allow you to 'question your teaspoons' or ask 'what is there under your wallpaper'.
>
> *(Highmore, 2000, p.43)*

Ben Highmore knows not only his Lefebvre and Certeau but also his Perec, which he uses here to speculate on an architecture that would challenge our perceptions of everyday life by 'getting in the way' and making us notice ordinary things. Perec would probably have argued against such an approach, as his central thesis was based on observing the world around us '...not to invent space [...] but to interrogate it'[36] (Perec, 1974).

Of course Highmore's speculation is ironical, but it has a serious side, and it could be argued that, for example, the work of architects Reversible Destiny / Shusaku Arakawa + Madeline Gins' 'architecture against death' (Arakawa and Gins, 1994) reflects some of this concern. Certainly their homes, with slopes and uneven floors, would make it difficult to stand up without great care, thus challenging the natural boredom that may arise out of a repetitive style of everydayness. And yet curiously, to the best of my knowledge, Arakawa and Gins were never associated or discussed in relation to the everyday, quite possibly because their architecture could be construed as just the opposite, an anti-everyday environment that

24 An everyday life approach to architecture

we can't help but notice. Highmore's tongue-in-cheek suggestion of a house that would 'disrupt the commodification of time and space, making such commodification unliveable' is a *fausse piste*. In other words, when Perec urges us to question our 'bricks, concrete, glass, our eating habits, our ustensils, our tools' (Perec, 2008, p.210), he doesn't ask for an architecture that gets in the way in order to be noticed. He pleads for a change of attitude towards questioning our everyday environment and our everyday life:

> It matters little to me that these questions should be fragmentary, barely indicative of a method, at most of a project. It matters a lot to me that they should seem trivial and futile: it's precisely what makes them just as essential, if not more, than many other questions through which we have tried in vain to capture our truth.
>
> *(Perec, 2008, p.211)*

By contrast to Arakawa and Gins, the Smithsons were firmly inducted in the 'everyday hall of fame' as alluded to in the previous section on As Found. For example, in Highmore's article on 'Patio and Pavilion', he posits that:

> The work of Alison and Peter Smithson has recently come in for renewed scrutiny, due in part to an upsurge of interest in the culture and politics of everyday life. Their association with the Independent Group in the 1950s, their critical interest in North American advertising, and their insistence that 'style' must be surrendered and swapped for a thorough engagement with the specificity of the architectural situation, have made them prime candidates for selection as the preeminent architects of the everyday.
>
> *(Highmore, 2006, p.271)*

Krucker's comments on the Smithsons' Upper Lawn house confirms this: 'The whole is rough, direct, and ordinary, but also highly sophisticated [...] the achievement and relevance of the Smithsons lies in the return of architecture to questions of reality and life' (Krucker, 2000, p.49),[37] reflecting Alison Smithson's own words

> 'In the late forties and early fifties when we first started thinking about housing, lack of identity, lack of any pattern of association, we used to talk of objects as found and anything and everything can be raised by association to become the poetry of the ordinary'.[38]

So if Alison and Peter Smithson were indeed the 'preeminent architects of the everyday', or at least re-interpreted as such after their death, who are the new 'architects of the everyday'? I may venture here that architects Jonathan Sergison and Stephen Bates[39] would have a strong claim to the title, together with 6A Architects – a self-proclaimed Practice of Everyday Life – unsurprising given Tom Emerson's enduring affection for Perec (Emerson, 2001). Difficult also not to mention 'Ordinary Architecture', founded in 2013 by Charles Holland and Elly Ward; the name of their practice refers to an interest in popular culture and an architecture that draws inspiration from the ordinary and the everyday.[40] And if Sergison Bates' architectural practice goes also some way to answer Frank-Bertholt Raith's question, 'Everyday architecture – in what style should we build?', I would suggest that Wigglesworth and Till's special issue of *AD* in 1998, *The Everyday and Architecture* provides an intellectual framework for architects to reflect on the everyday, in its post-Lefebvrian incarnation. In the introduction to *The Everyday and Architecture*, Wigglesworth and Till specify that they

> did not call the issue Architecture of the Everyday – because that would subsume the term into the canon of architecture and suggest that architecture can represent the everyday in a reified manner. The title *The Everyday and Architecture* is meant to provide a broader context in which to place the discussion and production of architecture.
>
> *(Wigglesworth and Till, 1998, p.7)*

This is a crucial point as it allows a much broader interpretation that covers both everyday life and the everyday environment, and their relationship, while Berke and Harris's book, *Architecture of the Everyday* (1997), is much more about the sort of question that was raised by Frank-Bertholt Raith. Wigglesworth and Till further point out that

> buildings, are inevitably involved in the vicissitudes of the everyday world. The problem arises when the actions of this world confront the isolated value system under which architecture is normally conceived – when repetitive practices occupy the one-off, when the humble street contains the monumental, when the minor event interrupts the grand narrative – when the kid with muddy boots drags herself across the pristine spaces of iconic modernism. Here the conceit is revealed. There is something inexorable about quotidian actions, which architecture is helpless to resist. Any discipline which denies the everyday will be denied everyday, and for this reason high architecture is unraveled by the habitual and banal events which mark the passage of time. There is a thudding disappointment as a gap opens up between the image of architecture and the reality of its making and occupation.
>
> *(Wigglesworth and Till, 1998, p.7)*

In the same *AD* issue, film-maker and architect Patrick Keiller writes on 'The Dilapidated Dwelling' and welcomes the revival of the notion of the everyday, in particular in relation to housing:

The notion of 'the everyday' in architecture offers a welcome relief from conventional interpretations of architectural value, especially in a culture where most 'everyday' building is not produced with much architectural intention, but it seems to affirm the spatial quality and detail of architects' architecture where it exists.

and again

For a long time, it had seemed that the spaces of everyday surroundings – the home, the high street and so on – were becoming more marginal in character, compared with other spaces that might be thought typically modern or postmodern – the airport, the office tower, the big museum and so on.

(Wigglesworth and Till, 1998, p.27)

Wigglesworth and Till paved the way for a discussion on the iconic versus the banal – the minor event versus the grand narrative – and the gap opening up between high architecture and its banal counterpart. This would be taken up at a later stage by Paul Finch as he states that:

Politicians should focus on the architecture of the everyday – and not on icons [...] Because design is so ubiquitous, you sometimes feel that politicians only think they have a responsibility when something is special, rather than everyday. But it is the everyday experience which, in aggregate, has the greatest effect on all our lives. Understanding this would be a good starting point for any future political strategy towards architecture and the built environment.

(AJ 28 August, 2013)

Finch might be stating the obvious, but it is a very seldom-expressed view, and he has the merit of bringing to the fore the urgency of the issue. Of course politicians could argue that the architectural press is equally guilty by featuring essentially iconic building projects.

But in the eyes of Shigeru Ban, architects are equally responsible, as he argued on receiving the 2014 Pritzker Prize: 'I was quite disappointed when I became an architect, because mostly we are working for privileged people who have money and power and we are hired to visualize their power and money with monumental architecture' (archdaily 2014). The same critique is levelled by McLeod against

[...] the escapism, heroism, and machismo of so much contemporary architectural thought. From the perspective of everyday life, such neo-avant-garde strategies as 'folding,' 'disjunction,' and 'bigness' deny the energy, humanity, and creativity embodied in the humble, prosaic details of daily existence. Architecture's 'star system' validates novelty and arrogance (even as big-name architects have become standardized and repetitive commodities), at the expense of what Lefebvre saw as the initial value of modernity: its relentless questioning of social life.

(Berke and Harris, 1997, p.27)

And given this context and background, one can only applaud the publication of the Farrell review of *Architecture + the Built Environment* (Farrell, 2014), a crucial document that was published in 2014[41] and for which Ed Vaizey, the Minister for Culture, Communications and Creative Industries in the Department for Culture, Media and Sport, praised Farrell's recommendations, citing 'a commitment to improving the everyday built environment and "making the ordinary better"' (Farrell, 2014, p.3). Unprecedentedly, the Farrell review 'champions the everyday above the one-off' (Farrell, 2014, p.128). While this may sound like grist to my mill as well as answering Paul Finch's prayers, there is only one mention of how it would affect people's lives:

With a new focus on everyday design, the media can begin to communicate to the public the potential positive impact of design decisions on daily life and help people better understand changes to the buildings and spaces with which they interact daily, such as their houses, high streets and parks.

(Farrell, 2014, p.54)

Unsurprisingly the review contains ample reference to the everyday, but to the everyday environment as opposed to everyday life. Still, it is a huge step forward and one suspects that it has been triggered by the housing crisis, in London in particular, and as remarked before the everyday and dwellings go hand in hand.

And improving the everyday built environment is a huge challenge, as our built environment is the product of innumerable forces:

Accidents [...] some happy, some not [...] clashes of scale and material, municipal idiocies and corporate boasts [...] these are some of the more salient determinants of our urban and suburban and extra-urban environments. Buildings are, of course, the major component of these environments. Some of those buildings will be the work of architects.

(Meades, 2012)

But the majority won't have been 'designed', resulting in a rather uninspiring environment according to Bishop

Place yourself in almost any urban setting outside of central London or the historic cores of many cities today and spin through 360 degrees: taking in the paving, the landscape, buildings, materials, positioning, planning, street furniture, streetscape and so on. Ask yourself: is there anything at all that isn't mediocre?

(Farrell, 2014, p.70)

This view doesn't concur with Venturi's opinion for whom 'main street was almost ok'!

The Farrell review and most architects writing about the everyday mean the everyday environment – but there is a need to focus on both forms of everyday, our environment and our life within it, as it is difficult to dissociate them since 'architecture's materiality makes it a natural conduit to the specificity of everyday life' (Upton, 2002, p.707). One is material, made of bricks, concrete and glass, while the other is immaterial and hard to define. The way around this conundrum is, for Upton, to derive a bodily approach to everyday life to 'arrive at a more concrete sense of the everyday, in every sense of the word. One definition of everyday life might be 'The nexus of spaces and times that repeatedly trigger bodily habits and cultural memories – the habitus' (Upton, 2002, p.720), the *habitus* being the concept defined by Bourdieu.[42]

Overall in this section we have traced the evolution of the notion of everyday life and noted that from the end of the 1990s onwards, the study of the everyday has shifted towards an interest in everyday architecture and everyday environment – as opposed to everyday life – boosted by the resurgence in housing, and with which the everyday is most strongly associated.

My own take is to study everyday life – once again not with a view to changing it – but to understand its relationship to architecture. Consequently I am not approaching 'everyday life through architecture' (Upton, 2002, p.707) but quite the reverse, as I am proposing to study architecture through the lens of everyday life. In other words, I am interested in examining everyday life in architecture as opposed to investigating architecture in everyday life. It would not make sense either to propose new forms of 'architecture of the everyday', although it is clearly an important field and relates to my own investigation, as this is the domain of practising architects. I am proposing here a new methodological approach by putting forward the idea that everyday life can be studied through the medium of film, and that doing so will throw new light on how we use architectural spaces – a much needed task given the lack of post-occupancy studies – helping to formulate new spatial understanding as well as to reveal new design possibilities.

Let us conclude this section with Lefebvre, for whom everyday space

[D]iffers from geometric space in that it has four dimensions, which are in a two-by-two opposition: 'right/left–high/low'. Similarly, everyday time has four dimensions which differ from dimensions as mathematicians and physicists would define them, namely the accomplished, the foreseen, the uncertain and the unforeseeable (or again: the past, the present, the short-term future and the long-term future).

(Lefebvre, 2014, p.525)

For Lefebvre this defines the social space, in which 'subjectively, social space is the environment of the group and of the individual within the group [...] Social space is made up of a relatively dense fabric of networks and channels. This fabric is an integral part of the everyday' (Lefebvre, 2014, p.525). Lefebvre's quasi-phenomenological definition of the relationship between everyday space and everyday time as subjective social space affords many permutations – a myriad of different forms of everyday life unravel within a multitude of combination of time and space. Those mechanisms are precisely at the heart of the film medium and are the subject of the next section.

Notes

1 Whenever I can I will be quoting from Lefebvre's *Critique of everyday life* in its three-volume text published by Verso in 2014. However for reasons of translation, I occasionally quote from the original French text of *Critique de la vie quotidienne* published in three separate volumes, in which case the translation will always be mine unless stated otherwise.

2 'In our opinion it is possible to formulate axioms in the social sciences and especially in sociology, but impossible to build any particular science using deductive theories (in other words, to establish a closed system by "saturating" that set of axioms)' (Lefebvre, 2014, p.394).

3 It should also be noted that Lefebvre did not regard the third volume of *Critique* as his last: 'in 1982, in an interview with Oliver Corpet and Thierry Paquot [...] Lefebvre indicated that he was planning to pursue this line of inquiry with a work on rhythms, revolving around the concept of "rhythm analysis" (Lefebvre, 2014, p.879). The project was realized only after his death, with the publication of *Elements de rythmanalyse. Introduction à la connaissance des rhythmes* (Lefebvre, 1992).

4 Michael Sheringham was one the finest commentators of the *quotidien* in the Anglo-Saxon world and his book is a key reading for anybody interested in the field (Sheringham, 2006).

5 French for please-insert or book summary or blurb, stuck at the very beginning of the book – almost as an afterthought.

6 My translation – original French text: *L'espace de notre vie n'est ni continu, ni infini, ni homogène, ni isotrope. Mais sait-on précisément où il se brise, où il se courbe, où il se déconnecte et où il se rassemble? On sent confusément des fissures, des hiatus, des points de friction, on a parfois la vague impression que ça coince quelque part, ou que ça éclate, ou que ça se cogne. Nous cherchons rarement à en savoir davantage et le plus souvent nous passons d'un endroit à l'autre, d'un espace à l'autre sans songer à mesurer, à prendre en charge, à prendre en compte ces laps d'espace. Le problème n'est pas d'inventer l'espace, encore moins de le ré-inventer (trop de gens bien intentionnés sont là aujourd'hui pour penser notre environnement...), mais de l'interroger, ou, plus simplement encore de le lire; car ce que nous appelons quotidienneté n'est pas évidence mais opacité: une forme de cécité, une manière d'anesthésie. C'est à partir de ces constatations élémentaires que s'est développé ce livre, journal d'un usager de l'espace* (Perec, 1974).

7 'Ce qui se passe vraiment, ce que nous vivons, le reste, tout le reste, où est il ? Ce qui se passe chaque jour et qui revient chaque jour, le banal, le quotidien, l'évident, le commun, l'ordinaire, l'infra-ordinaire, le bruit de fond, l'habituel, comment en rendre compte, comment l'interroger, comment le décrire? [...] Peut-être s'agit-il de fonder enfin notre propre anthropologie: celle qui parlera de nous,

30 An everyday life approach to architecture

qui ira chercher en nous ce que nous avons si longtemps pillé chez les autres. Non plus l'exotique, mais l'endotique' (Perec, 1989, pp.11–12).

8 For more information see Kristin Ross' interview with Henri Lefebvre in 1983 on his relationship with the situationists (Ross and Lefebvre, 1997).

9 *L'Ouvroir de littérature potentielle* (Oulipo), was founded in 1960 by Raymond Queneau and François Le Lionnais, and aimed to discover, propose and invent literary *contraintes* as an aid to potential new forms of writing. Amongst the members of l'Oulipo were Italo Calvino, Jacques Roubaud, Raymond Queneau, and Georges Perec – for further information see James, 2006.

10 Perec on *la contrainte*: '*Contrainte et liberté sont des fonctions indissociables de l'oeuvre : la contrainte n'est pas ce qui interdit la liberté, la liberté n'est pas ce qui n'est pas contrainte ; au contraire, la contrainte est ce qui permet la liberté, la liberté est ce qui surgit de la contrainte*' (Perec, 1993).

11 In the preface to the third volume of *Critique*, Michel Trebitsch summarizes the relationship between the two men as follows: 'According to Eleonore Kofman and Elizabeth Lebas, having established contact through the New Left milieu in 1958 with the young Georges Perec, who at the time was doing his military service, Lefebvre employed him on various studies in Normandy and the Oise. A friendship was born out of this and Perec subsequently stayed on several occasions at Navarrenx, Lefebvre's house in the Pyrenees, which is where he probably became fully committed to becoming a writer'. Hence this was a significant encounter for both men, as Perec's biographer David Bellos has emphasized, involving mutual influence, as demonstrated by recent work in the context of the seminar of the Georges Perec association at the University of Paris VII. Thus, in his *Introduction to Modernity* (1962), Lefebvre draws a parallel between Ligne générale, a small avant-garde group to which Perec belonged, and the Situationist group as one of the spearheads of a 'new romanticism' that was revolutionary in character. Above all, he refers to Perec's oeuvre, especially *Les Choses* (1965), several times in *Everyday Life in the Modern World*. As for Perec, the influence of *Critique of Everyday Life* and, more generally, of Lefebvre's thinking on alienation, on the cult of objects and commodities, on the banal, and on the 'infra-ordinary', finds numerous echoes not only in *Les Choses*, but also in *Un homme qui dort* (1967), and even *Espèces d'espaces* (1974) (Lefebvre, 2014, p.658).

12 I had long lost my own handouts but I am most grateful for Giles Leresche to have retrieved the notes that our mutual friend Jean-Pierre Courtillot had left with him all those years!

13 For more information, the section on 'Lefebvre and the Architects' is extremely informative and well documented (see pp.27–48).

14 *Le droit à la ville* was translated and edited by Kofman and Lebas as *Writing on Cities* (Lefebvre, 1996).

15 In *Le droit à la ville*, Lefebvre states that '*Le droit à la ville ne peut se concevoir comme un simple droit de visite ou de retour vers les villes traditionnelles. Il ne peut se formuler que comme droit à la vie urbaine, transformée, renouvelée*'. [...] He goes on to berate '*la nouvelle aristocratie bourgeoise [...] ils fascinent les gens plongés dans le quotidien; ils transcendent la quotidienné [...]*'. Lefebvre argues that '*les olympiens*' live in the centre, while the working class has been shifted to the periphery: '*Il suffit d'ouvrir les yeux pour comprendre la vie quotidienne de celui qui court de son logement à la gare proche ou lointaine, au métro bondé, au bureau ou à l'usine, pour reprendre le soir ce même chemin, et venir chez lui récupérer la force de recommencer le lendemain*' (Lefebvre, 2009, p.108).

Lefebvre sees the city and *Le droit à la ville* as the social space from which to radically reinvent the everyday for the working class, so that they too would have a right to the city as opposed to living in the suburbs – we also have to note that *Le droit à la ville* was published in March 1968, and it has been suggested that it had an influence on the May 1968 events: '*L'impact du* Droit à la ville *peut difficilement être évalué dans le déclenchement de cet évènement [i.e May 68]. Il a tout de même largement participé à la prise de conscience que la vie quotidienne était loin d'être déterminée par le travail, car elle se situait « ailleurs » dans la ville. Ces thèmes ont été repris lors des manifestations ; les slogans du type « métro, boulot, dodo », « HLM blêmes » reprenaient sa dénonciation de la fabrication de l'anti-ville. Ces évènements marquaient, selon lui, l'appropriation de l'espace par les masses populaires à travers l'action des étudiants qui a servi de « catalyseur, d'analyseur révélateur ». Cet enthousiasme reposait sur l'idée ou l'illusion (?) que l'on assistait alors, concrètement, à la réalisation de l'implication de la classe ouvrière comme avant-garde qui investit le terrain des luttes urbaines et qui, enfin, allait préparer et garantir, par son action, le droit à la ville'* (Costes, 2010, p.182).

16 In 1981 Perec gave a conference in Albi entitled 'A propos de la description' [regarding the description] as part of a colloquium on *Espace et representation* (20–24 July 1981), organized by Alain Renier (président du Laboratoire d'architecture no 1 de l'Unité pédagogique d'architecture n°6 in Paris). This seminar was later transcribed and published (Bertelli and Ribière, 2003, pp.227–243).

17 'L'inhabitable [...] les villes nauséabondes. L'inhabitable : l'architecture du mépris et de la frime, la gloriole médiocre des tours et des buildings, les milliers de cagibis entassés les uns au-dessus des autres [...] L'inhabitable : les bidonvilles, les villes bidon [...]'

18 A summary of current trends and experiments in architecture, geography and urban studies, based on Perec's *l'architexteur*, can be found in *Espèces d'Espace Perecquiens*, the twelfth volume of the Cahiers Georges Perec (Constantin, Danielle et al., 2015). I have myself used Perec's methods of urban observation in various studio contexts using film (Penz, 2012).

19 Manning Durdin Robertson was an Irish town planner, architect and writer – and when I first borrowed his book from the Cambridge University Library, I discovered that I was the first to consult it since 1924...such was the interest in everyday architecture!

20 The true purpose of Robertson's book, which is not irrelevant here, was intended 'principally for those who so far have not interested themselves in the beauty or ugliness of their surroundings, in the hope that it may set up a train of thought in the mind of the ordinary practical individual that will help to reintroduce into everyday life some of the interest and beauty we will all associate with the traditional architecture of the old English village and cathedral city, but which we neither expect nor find in our modern towns and suburbs' (Robertson, 1924, p.13). In other words, Manning Robertson produced one of the first books about the appreciation of vernacular architecture but also became interested in more modern developments such as The White Hart Lane Estate – masterminded by G. Topham Forrest and in effect London County Council's first 'garden suburb' – and in which he saw a pioneering housing scheme that might 'secure our release from monotonous and depressing surroundings' (Robertson, 1924, p.23). He was probably a 'closet modernist', hoping for a better everyday English suburban architecture – in that sense he was himself a pioneer whom the Smithsons might have approved of or have been inspired by, although history does not relate.

21 My translation from the French: *250 millions ont été consacrés à la recherche dans tous les domaines de l'habitat, y compris le "sociologique": fait capital et caractéristique originale du Plan Construction.*

22 Luce Giard was a close collaborator of de Certeau and edited Vols 1 and 2 of *L'invention du quotidien* (De Certeau, 1990).

23 Maffesoli had published a year before de Certeau *La conquête du present: pour une sociologie de la vie quotidienne* (1979).

24 According to Sheringham, '*Construire pour habiter* acknowledges the everyday, but just as importantly it recognizes that by this point in French cultural history, the turn of the 1980s, a body of ideas and a set of discourses on the *quotidien*, associated with Perec, Lefebvre, Certeau and others, were available to articulate and inspire new insights into everyday life' (Sheringham, 2006, p.2).

25 On the issue of translation, Sheringham further commented that 'In all cases the hazards of translation impact on reception, leading, in Lefebvre's case, to a serious distortion of his thinking on the everyday. The English translation of the first volume of the *Critique de la vie quotidienne* did not appear until 1991, prior to which the main source was the less representative synthesis Lefebvre wrote in 1968, *La vie quotidienne dans le monde moderne*, immediately translated as *Everyday Life in the Modern World*', further adding that 'the absence, until 2002, of an English translation of the second, 1961, volume of Lefebvre's *Critique* means that the full flowering of his thoughts on the *quotidien* has been

32 An everyday life approach to architecture

ignored by "cultural studies", impeding understanding of its true relation to the work of Certeau' (Sheringham, 2006, p.7).

26 We also have to note that Lefebvre's urban studies work is in general better known in the anglo-saxon world than his work on the everyday as highlighted by Claire Revol, see (Revol, 2012, p.105–106).

27 It is useful to acknowledge that in 1987, a special issue on Everyday Life was published in the journal of Yale French Studies (ed. Ross, Kristin and Alice Kaplan), in which Lefebvre wrote *The Everyday and Everydayness* (Lefebvre and Levich, 1987), which was a translation of *Quotidien et Quotidienneté* that Lefebvre had written for the Encyclopedia Universalis.

28 Stierli remarks in his excellent book, *Las Vegas in the Rearview Mirror*, that 'it is an important milestone in contemporary architectural history and that the methods of urban analysis systematically presented in the work for the first time continue to exert a defining influence on architectural and urbanist thinking to this day. In this respect Scott Brown recently observed that "Las Vegas is not a standard for future growth. It is a standard for conceptual analysis"' (Stierli, 2013, p.19).

29 Stierli also co-curated the *Las Vegas* exhibition at the 2015 *Les Rencontres d'Arles* (Stadler and Stierli, 2015), a photographic exhibition which I was able to visit and where I saw first hand all the *deadpan* films.

30 Fausch further reminds us that '"Concrete, direct observation and notation of ordinary, everyday experience" played an important part in Venturi and Scott Brown's program of investigation. Reiterating Le Corbusier's diatribe against "eyes which do not see" the beauties of vernacular and standardized industrial construction, *Learning from Las Vegas* emphasized the need to "question how we look at things" in an "open-minded and nonjudgmental investigation," and to use both old and new techniques for documenting the details of the new urban forms' (Berke and Harris, 1997, p.95).

31 'Denise discovered Ed Ruscha when she taught at UCLA in the mid-1960s and we both had been learning from the Pop artists and their appreciation of the everyday from the late 1950s on' (Stierli, 2013, p.147).

32 According to Fausch: 'The connections between Venturi and Scott Brown's theoretical work during this period and that of the Smithsons have often been noted. Along with the Smithsons, Independent Group members Nigel and Judith Henderson's sociological and photographic observations questioned the premises of (upper-middle-class) socialist architecture after World War II. Reyner Banham's discussions of popular culture, and especially Los Angeles, also arose out of this milieu. Although Peter Smithson was not yet teaching at the Architectural Association when Scott Brown was a student there, she has described her relationships with student groups who held points of view similar to those being propounded by the Independent Group in its exhibits Parallel of Life and Art and This is Tomorrow. Scott Brown also used Peter Smithson as an informal critic for her thesis' (Berke and Harris, 1997, p.95).

33 In 1945 the Hendersons moved to Bethnal Green because Judith Henderson was the anthropologist in charge of the *Discover Your Neighbour* project. While her research was broadly in keeping with the Mass Observation movement, it consisted of a series of in-depth case studies in which she observed and recorded the lives of neighbouring families. Judith Henderson's anthropological approach and her corresponding perspective were a decisive influence on her husband's photographic activities. Self-taught as a photographer, he documented Bethnal Green from 1947 to 1952 (Lichtenstein and Schregenberger, 2001, p.84). Stierli also points out Henderson's influence on Denise Scott Brown, who 'paid particular attention to the everyday dwellings and environment of regular people. In this regard, she could draw upon Nigel Henderson's photographs of London's East End, which were familiar to her from her time "studying in London"' (Stierli, 2013, p.110).

34 At a push one can fathom a tenuous link by means of the Mass Observation movement, through Henderson in the first place, and for which Hubble posits that 'there are strong reasons for considering Mass Observation within the growing sub-discipline of "Everyday Life" Studies' (Hubble, 2006, p.11).

35 Interesting to note that Lefebvre mentions in the section on young workers and factory life 'the excellent film *Saturday Night and Sunday Morning*' (Reisz, 1960) – footnote 22 – (Lefebvre, 2014, p.869).

36 My translation from the French in *le prière d'insérer*: '*Le problème n'est pas d'inventer l'espace, encore moins de le ré-inventer (trop de gens bien intentionnés sont là aujourd'hui pour penser notre environnement...), mais de l'interroger, ou, plus simplement encore de le lire*'.

37 In fact there are no less than two articles in *Daidalos* – out of 13 – about the Smithsons – the other one being by Irénée Scalbert.

38 A quote from Alison Smithson in a BBC documentary *The Smithsons on Housing* (1970), made by B.S. Johnson, in which both Alison and Peter Smithson are interviewed.

39 They wrote an article in the special issue of *Daidalos* on The Everyday (Sergison and Bates, 2000) and in 2003 in a special issue of *L'Architecture d'Aujourd'hui* dedicated to the Smithsons, they contributed a section entitled 'Six lessons learnt from Alison and Peter Smithson' in which there is a part on the *As found* – one of the six lessons, stating that 'The essence of *as found* as a concept lies in the acceptance of the value of the everyday [...] The concept of *as found* has encouraged us to open our eyes to all that lies around us' (Sergison and Bates, 2003, p.81). Sergison went on to write a piece entitled 'Reflections on the house and the city', in a special issue of *Block* entitled 'The Modest', making the point that 'In our work in the field of housing we have always resisted the pressure to be spectacular. On the contrary our work is often accused of being "quiet". While we do not take this as a compliment we hold a strong conviction that housing should be decent and carefully considered but have a gentle relationship to the normative. We argue that the image we give a building should not impose pressure on future inhabitants to perform according to the designer's social projections. This is why we try and employ an architectural language that we hope will seem familiar' (Sergison, 2010, p.16). There is no doubt that Sergison and Bates have inherited from the Smithsons the *as found/everyday* mantle – most evident in their public housing projects – a building type which is the natural milieu for the everyday to flourish in. While there could be a tendency for architects 'to try to incorporate the everyday into their work, the results tend to be embarrassingly literal and decorative' (Upton, 2002, p.73), this is not the case with Sergison Bates, as they have rediscovered and re-interpreted the *as found* in a subtle and effective way.

40 The following extract from their website defines further their position: 'What is ordinary architecture? For us it means a number of things. Architecture itself is profoundly ordinary. Unlike most art forms, architecture is encountered in the everyday, in a "blur of habit". We use buildings all the time without necessarily appreciating their aesthetic or formal qualities, at least not overtly. Architecture is mostly a backdrop to everyday life rather than its focus' [www.ordinaryarchitecture.co.uk/writing-a-life-more-ordinary/4590281652].

41 Farrell recalls in its introduction 'In January 2013 Ed Vaizey, Minister for Culture, Communications and the Creative Industries, asked me to undertake a national review of architecture and the built environment. I have undertaken this Review independently with my team at Farrells and advised by a panel of 11 industry leaders with a breadth of experience that covers education, outreach, urbanism, architecture, property and philosophy'.

42 Upton elaborates further that 'The anthropologist Pierre Bourdieu saw this clearly. Everyday life is not a system of representations or performances, he wrote, but a "system of structured, structuring dispositions ... which is constituted in practice and is always oriented toward practical functions." He called this system the *habitus*, or practical sense' (Upton, 2002, p.719).

References

Allain-Dupré Fabry, E. & Lavalou, A. (1981) *Construire pour Habiter*. Paris: Editions l'Equerre – Plan Construction.

34 An everyday life approach to architecture

Arakawa & Gins, M. (1994) *Architecture: sites of reversible destiny: (architectural experiments after Auschwitz-Hiroshima)*. Art and design monograph. London: Academy Editions.

archdaily.com www.archdaily.com/490336/video-charlie-rose-interviews-tom-pritzker-and-shigeru-ban

Bachelard, G. (1957) *La poétique de l'espace*. Bibliothèque de philosophie contemporaine. Paris: Presses universitaires de France.

Benjamin, W. (2007) *Illuminations*. Hannah Arendt (ed.). New York: Schocken Books.

Berke, D. & Harris, S. (1997) *Architecture of the Everyday*. 1st edition. Princeton Architectural Press.

Bertelli, D. & Ribière, M. (eds) (2003) *Entretiens et conférences / Georges Perec*. Nantes: Joseph K.

Blanchot, M. & Hanson, S. (1987) Everyday Speech. *Yale French Studies*. (73), 12.

Confurius, G. (ed.) (2000) 'The everyday', in *Daidalos*. Berlin: pp. 4–97.

Constantin, D. et al. (eds.) (2015) *Espèces d'Espace Perecquiens*. Cahiers Georges Perec. Vol. 12. Bordeaux: Le Castor Astral.

Costes, L. (2010) Le Droit à la ville de Henri Lefebvre : quel héritage politique et scientifique ? *Espaces et sociétés*. 140–141 (1), 177.

De Certeau, M. (1990) *L'invention du quotidien*. Collection Folio/essais 146, 238. Nouv. éd. Paris: Gallimard.

Emerson, T. (2001) From Lieux to Life… *AA Files*. (45/46), 92–97.

Farrell, T. (2014) *The Farrell review of Architecture and the Built Environment*. [online]. Available from: www.farrellreview.co.uk

Highmore, B. (2000) 'Dwelling on the Daily: On the term everyday life as used by Henri Lefebvre and Michel de Certeau', in Gerrit Confurius (ed.) *The everyday*. Berlin: Daidalos. pp. 38–43.

Highmore, B. (2006) Rough Poetry: Patio and Pavilion Revisited. *Oxford Art Journal*. 29 (2), 269–290.

Hubble, N. D. (2006) *Mass-Observation and Everyday Life: Culture, History, Theory*. 2006 edition. Houndmills, Basingstoke, Hampshire; New York: AIAA.

James, A. (2006) Pour un modèle diagrammatique de la contrainte : l'écriture oulipienne de Georges Perec. *Cahiers de l'Association internationale des études francaises*. 58 (1), 379–404.

Krucker, B. (2000) 'Complex Ordinariness. The Upper-Lawn Pavilion', in Gerrit Confurius (ed.) *The everyday*. Berlin: Daidalos. pp. 44–51.

Kuhn, A. & Westwell, G. (2012) *A Dictionary of Film Studies*. 1st edition. Oxford University Press [online]. Available from: www.oxfordreference.com/view/10.1093/acref/9780199587261.001. 0001/acref-9780199587261 (Accessed 25 April 2016).

Lefebvre, H. (1958) *Critique de la vie quotidienne – Vol. 1 – Introduction. Le sens de la marche* [2. éd.]. Paris: L'Arche.

Lefebvre, H. (1986) *La production de l'espace*. 3e éd. Paris: Anthropos.

Lefebvre, H. (1992) *Eléments de rythmanalyse: introduction à la connaissance des rythmes*. Collection explorations et découvertes en terres humaines. René. Lourau (ed.). Paris: Editions Syllepse.

Lefebvre, H. (1996) *Writings on cities*. Eleonore Kofman & Elizabeth Lebas (eds.). Oxford: Blackwell Publishers.

Lefebvre, H. (2009) *Le droit à la ville*. Anthropologie. 3e éd. Paris: Economica: Anthropos.

Lefebvre, H. (2014) *Critique of everyday life*. The three-volume text. London: Verso.

Lefebvre, H. & Levich, C. (1987) The everyday and everydayness. *Yale French Studies*. (73), 7–11.

Lichtenstein, C. & Schregenberger, T. (2001) *As Found: The Discovery of the Ordinary British Architecture and Art of the 1950s: Independent Group and New Brutalism*. Lars Muller Publishers.

Meades, J. (2012) Jonathan Meades: Architects are the last people who should shape our cities. *The Guardian*. 18 September [online]. Available from: www.theguardian.com/artanddesign/2012/sep/18/ architects-cities-jonathan-meades (Accessed 7 September 2016).

Penz, F. (2012) Towards an Urban Narrative Layers Approach to Decipher the Language of City Films. *Comparative Literature and Culture*. 14 (3) [online]. Available from: http://docs.lib.purdue.edu/ clcweb/vol14/iss3/7/ (Accessed 28 April 2016).

Perec, G. (1974) *Espèces d'espaces*. Espace critique. Paris: Galilée.

Perec, G. (1989) *L'infra-ordinaire*. La librairie du XXe siècle. Paris: Seuil.

Perec, G. (1993) Georges Perec. *Magazine Littéraire*. (316).

Perec, G. (2003) *Penser/Classer*. Paris: Seuil: La Librairie du XXe siècle.

Perec, G. (2008) *Species of Spaces and Other Pieces (Penguin Classics)*. Penguin Classics.

Peytard, J. (1997) 'De l'écriture-calligramme à l'écriture-cinéma: le cas Perec', in *Le Cabinet d'amateurs – Revue d'études perecquiennes*. Presses universitaires du Mirail-Toulouse.

Raith, F.-B. (2000) 'Everyday architecture – in what style should we build?', in Gerrit Confurius (ed.) *The everyday*. Berlin: Daidalos. pp. 7–16.

Read, A. (ed.) (2000) *Architecturally speaking: practices of art, architecture and the everyday*. London: Routledge.

Revol, C. (2012) 'Le succès de Lefebvre dans les urban studies anglo-saxonnes et les conditions de sa redécouverte en France', in *L'Homme et la société*. Paris: L'Harmattan. pp. 105–118.

Robertson, M. (1924) *Everyday architecture*. New York: McDevitt-Wilson's.

Roche, A. (2015) 'Perec et les "faiseurs de ville"', in Danielle Constantin et al. (eds.) *Espèces d'Espace Perecquiens*. Cahiers Georges Perec. Bordeaux: Le Castor Astral.

Ross, K. & Lefebvre, H. (1997) Lefebvre on the Situationists: An Interview. *October*. 7969–7983.

Rossi, A. (2010) *A Scientific Autobiography*. MIT Press [online]. Available from: www.amazon.co.uk/ Scientific-Autobiography-Oppositions-Books-Rossi/dp/0262514389.

Schilling, D. (2006) *Mémoires du quotidien: les lieux de Perec*. La collection Perspectives. Villeneuve d'Ascq: Presses universitaires du Septentrion.

Sergison, J. (2010) 'Reflections on the house and the city', in Rob Wilson (ed.) *Block. Issue 1: The Modest*.

Sergison, J. & Bates, S. (2000) 'More Tolerance. A public house and housing', in Gerrit Confurius (ed.) *The Everyday*. Berlin: Daidalos. pp. 28–37.

Sergison, J. & Bates, S. (2003) Six lessons learnt from Alison & Peter Smithson [text in French and English]. *Architecture d'Aujourd'hui*. (No. 344), 74–81.

Sheringham, M. (2006) *Everyday life: theories and practices from surrealism to the present*. Oxford: Oxford University Press.

Stadler, H. & Stierli, M. (eds.) (2015) *Las Vegas Studio: Images from the Archive of Robert Venturi and Denise Scott Brown*. Zürich: Scheidegger & Spiess.

Stanek, Ł. (2011) *Henri Lefebvre on space: architecture, urban research, and the production of theory*. Minneapolis: University of Minnesota Press.

Stierli, M. (2013) *Las Vegas in the rearview mirror: the city in theory, photography, and film*. Los Angeles: Getty Research Institute.

Tschumi, B. (2004) Avant-Propos: Bernard Tschumi in Conversation with Enrique Walker. *Grey Room*. (17), 118–126.

Upton, D. (2002) Architecture in Everyday Life. *New Literary History*. 33 (4), 707–723.

Venturi, R. et al. (1972) *Learning from Las Vegas*. Cambridge, Mass.: MIT Press.

Wigglesworth, S. & Till, J. (1998) *Architecture of the Everyday*. London: John Wiley & Sons.

PART 2

Everydayness and cinema

2
INTRODUCTION TO EVERYDAYNESS AND CINEMA

The implied claim is that film, the latest of the great arts, shows philosophy to be the often invisible accompaniment of the ordinary lives that film is so apt to capture.

Stanley Cavell (2005, p.6)

Having concluded the last section with Lefebvre's remarks on space and time, let us restart with some of his thinking on cinema. In the second volume of *Critique*, Lefebvre writes:

Let us emphasize yet again the efforts which literature, cinema and even some specialists in the social sciences have made to get closer to the 'lived', to eliminate the arbitrary transpositions of the everyday, to grasp 'what is extraordinary within the ordinary', and 'the significance of the insignificant'. Questions of the value of this or that novel or film or aesthetic theory apart, all this proves the validity of a critical study of everyday life.

(Lefebvre, 2014, p.298)

Lefebvre cites here as an example *Chronique d'un été,* directed by Jean Rouch and Edgar Morin in 1962 (Lefebvre, 2014, p.358). It was a key film that attempted to uncover the everyday, alongside Debord's own efforts, using a documentary style known as *cinema-verité.* As McDonough remarks,

Chronique d'un été was a film, then, whose subject was everyday life itself, that rather unformed, amorphous daily existence and its imbrication with (or disjunction from) the broader world and the forces of history. And as such, it was by no means unique: at the same moment when *Chronique* was being filmed in Paris, Guy Debord was shooting his short film, *Critique de la séparation* (Critique of Separation) [...] he, too, was concerned with investigating everyday life.

(McDonough, 2007, p.7)

Some of the DNA of this film movement can be traced back to Soviet film-maker Dziga-Vertov, as *cinema-verité is a direct translation of* Vertov's *kino-pravda* (film-truth) – but there are marked differences.[1]

Lefebvre's writing on film is minimal but nevertheless encouraging, and the idea that cinema may get us closer to the 'lived' experience is helpful in this context. Cultural studies scholars of Lefebvre have further commented on film's validity as a tool in the study of everyday life. For example, Sheringham draws on a range of films by Godard, Akerman, Rouch & Morin, arguing that they provide 'the relational, performative aspects of the *quotidien* – a dimension that emerges through the act of being apprehended – are enacted in the way a film, a play or artwork "stages" an interaction between human subject and social structure' (Sheringham, 2006, p.334).[2] Similarly Kristin Ross states that

If I return throughout the book to the films of Jacques Tati, it is because they make palpable a daily life that increasingly appeared to unfold in a space where objects tended to dictate to people their gestures and movements – gestures that had not yet congealed into any degree of rote familiarity, and that for the most part had to be learned from watching American films.

(Ross, 1996, p.11)

But while Lefebvre, Sheringham and Ross appear to give credibility to part of my initial hypothesis, they do not specifically consider the everydayness of the built environment but everyday life in general. And they only use cinema in restricted parts of their studies. On the other hand, Patrick Keiller, coming from a tradition of filmmaking and architecture, suggests an interesting connection:

For anyone in pursuit of, let's say, the improvement of everyday life, a medium which offers a heightened awareness of architecture – the medium of film – might be thought at least as compelling as an actually existing architecture of heightened awareness – an ecstatic architecture, whatever that might be.

(Keiller, 2013, p.84)

Similarly, Peter Halley remarks on the everyday found in

...the progressive American cinema of *The Last Picture Show*, *Midnight Cowboy*, and *Badlands*. It is the everyday of sunlight, of the periphery, of the unnoticed [...] at which time seems to slow down, daily concerns dissipate, and our senses become receptive to sight and sound.

(Berke and Harris, 1997, p.191)

Certainly Keiller is going further than I had originally anticipated as he suggests linking cinema with an 'improvement' of daily life, not unlike Lefebvre's project seeking to change the everyday. But I also start from the premise of an observation of the world around me – in all its everydayness, and I would situate this work within the methodological line traced by Kevin Lynch (Lynch, 1960), William Holly Whyte (Whyte, 2001), Venturi and Scott Brown (Venturi, Scott Brown, and Izenour, 1972). As to the question – does the study and observation of films, once removed from the 'real', make us 'passive observers' as opposed to 'active participants'? – one should construe this as a phase, part of a much wider creative process, enriched by this practice. It isn't an end in itself. This is where both Lefebvre's and Keiller's remarks about changing everydayness start to make sense. For Keiller 'the improvement of everyday life through the medium' of film happens on at least two levels: he sees in the film medium the opportunity to not only observe but also make suggestions. For example, his film *The Dilapidated Dwelling* (2000) contributes to the debate on housing, but also the images themselves, through the framing, choice of location and camera set-up, constitute a potentially powerful visual analysis of the city. In the same way as Venturi learned from Las Vegas, we can also 'learn from London' through Keiller's film *London* (1994). In other words, cinema contains large chunks of everydayness of the type that we do not pay much attention to in our own daily life but which may be useful to designers. Cinema is a form of spatial practice, for example of domestic situations, and while not all films are useful to study, most contain a large amount of information that can be drawn from them.

The everyday and the realism argument

Architects don't invent anything, they transform reality.

Alvaro Siza (Slessor, 2015)

My films are like wine, or bread. It's all real. But during the process of winemaking or breadmaking, the original materials get transformed into something else. So I extract little fragments of reality and I make something different out of them.

(Mekas, 2010, p.15)[3]

This process of transformation evoked by Mekas – and Siza – makes the issue of realism[4] in film a complex subject, and although it is not central to my argument, it is useful here to air it in relation to everyday life – and how it connects to cinema. For this we must turn yet again to

Lefebvre who raises, particularly in Volume 1 of *Critique*, some interesting issues in relation to realism. 'The display of luxury to be seen in so many films, most of them mediocre,[5] takes on an almost fascinating character, and the spectator is uprooted from his everyday world by an everyday world other than his own'. Importantly Lefebvre acknowledges here the recreation in film of another everyday world, one that the spectators are invited to enter and that differs from their own everyday reality – he refers to it as *l'étrangeté familière du rêve* – the strange familiarity of dreams (Lefebvre, 1958, p.16).

Further, in the section devoted to Charlie Chaplin and Bertolt Brecht,[6] and moving away from 'mediocre' films, Lefebvre notes that 'Happily, contemporary cinema and theatre have other works to offer which reveal a truth about everyday life' (Lefebvre, 2014, p.32). Here Lefebvre implies that film can provide some sort of revelation concerning everyday life, and he chooses Chaplin as an example to illustrate his thinking: 'Chaplin's first films may be seen as offering a critique of everyday life: a critique in action, a basically optimistic critique, with the living, human unity of its two faces, the negative and the positive. Hence its "success"' (Lefebvre, 2014, p.33). While still referring to Chaplin, he sees that his films present us with '[…] an image of everyday reality, taken in its totality or as a fragment, reflecting that reality in all its depth through people, ideas and things which are apparently quite different from everyday experience and therefore exceptional, deviant, abnormal' (Lefebvre, 2014, p.33).

In other words, Lefebvre comes to the conclusion that although Chaplin's films may at first appear to be offering a valid critique of everyday life, in the end they portray a different reality from ordinary life – precisely because the character portrayed by Chaplin, typically the tramp (*l'homme aberrant*), stands outside of everyday life[7] and therefore belongs to the 'exceptional' category. Thus his films reverse what Lefebvre originally valued in cinema by eliciting 'what is ordinary within the extraordinary'. For Lefebvre, Chaplin's films present us with a 'reverse image'.[8] While it might appear that Lefebvre is using a counterexample, he is in fact opposing Chaplin and Brecht over the reverse image, through two forms of representation of everyday life, and particular ones at that, and favours Brecht's anti-realist[9] approach, despite having some reservations[10] (Lefebvre, 2014, p.45). Lefebvre is also critical of so-called 'realist' authors and film and theatre directors[11] who, being incapable of extracting the extraordinary out of the ordinary, concentrate instead on trying to make ordinary and banal events interesting, in effect colouring *la grisaille* of people's lives.[12]

But Lefebvre ventures a way forward.[13] He hypothesizes how the banal could be taken out of its ordinary setting – *dégagé de son contexte* – and he takes the example of the humble plant or weed which, extracted from the earth and considered closely, acquires a new meaning and becomes a marvel (*une merveille*). Lefebvre acknowledges the difficulty of creating a convincing montage of such images, as they would need to be extracted out of their everyday life context, while at the same time being quintessentially representative of their quotidian milieu, but concluded that this is a possible approach for an everyday realism – putting forward as successful examples (Lefebvre, 2014, p.36) of such an approach, Fellini's *La Strada* (1954) and *Salt of the Earth*[14] (Biberman, 1954).

In doing so, Lefebvre appears to have rediscovered the lessons of Fernand Léger:

> 80% of the elements and objects that help us to live are only perceived by us in our everyday lives, while 20% are actually seen [and taken notice of]. From this, I deduce the cinematographic revolution is to make us see everything that has been merely caught sight of... The dog that goes by in the street is only perceived. Projected on the screen, it is seen, so much so that the whole audience reacts as if it discovered the dog for the first time [...] that's the value of framing an image judiciously. Bear this in mind – this is the crux of this new art form.
>
> *(Léger, 1922)*[15]

The two examples of the plant and the dog intimate that as the camera frames reality it reveals and makes us 'see' what is otherwise overlooked. So in a curious way, if we accept what Léger states, film simplifies reality – it makes us notice things, it directs our gaze. So within the realm of everyday life, film helps us to notice and grasp a 'reality' to which we are otherwise blind. Indeed, life itself is hard to grasp and discern in what Lukács called 'the chiaroscuro of everyday life'[16] where 'Life is an anarchy of light and dark' (Lukács, 1974, pp.152,153). On the other hand, cinema makes a complex reality more accessible to us – because of the framing but also the editing and the montage. It draws our attention to what we would normally not pay attention to. It has our undivided attention, which is particularly true when we experience it in the cinema, allowing us to concentrate fully on 'the big picture', the action or drama, whatever that might be, as well as cinephiliac moments, marginal filmic details.[17] But we also know that in order to study the everyday life component of a film, if we want to appreciate fiction films for their documentary revelations about the quotidian, several viewings will be necessary, clearly not all taking place in a cinema.

And yet there are clear difficulties ahead in grasping the everyday in film. Adorno warns that

> If the film were to give itself up to the blind representation of everyday life, following the precepts of, say, Zola, as would indeed be practicable with moving photography and sound recording, the result would be a construction alien to the visual habits of the audience, diffuse, unarticulated outwards. Radical naturalism, to which the technique of film lends itself, would dissolve all surface coherence of meaning and finish up as the antithesis of familiar[18] realism.
>
> *(Adorno, 2005, pp.141–142)*

Adorno here rejoins Lefebvre (and Brecht) in shunning movies depicting bland and ordinary everyday life with no extraordinary elements within it. Adorno argues that the habit of the viewer tends towards a form of 'familiar realism', say for example an average Hollywood movie, familiar to us all, while 'radical naturalism' would be disturbing for an audience.[19]

David Trotter's own reading of Lukács[20] confirms that naturalism moves away from narrative as 'Narrative binds event to event, as cause to effect, and so produces meaning. Description unbinds. Lukács enables us to understand Naturalism[21] as a formal lowering, from narrative into description' (Trotter, 2008, p.153).

However, the close association of the everyday with naturalist films (Kuhn and Westwell, 2012) is far from obvious for Andrew Klevan, in his excellent and rather unique study of the everyday in film[22] – *Disclosure of the everyday: The undramatic achievements in Narrative film* (Klevan, 1996), as he posits that

> Naturalistic films might achieve a more authentic affinity to aspects of reality, but not necessarily with regard to those features associated with the uneventful which I have taken to be characteristic of the everyday [...] the pursuit of the 'more real', the seeking of styles and scenarios with a more natural resemblance to life (which has taken a variety of forms), has often produced varieties of anomalous melodrama rather than led to more accurate depictions of the everyday.
>
> *(Klevan, 1996, p.47)*

Klevan identifies the uneventful to be the main characteristic of the everyday, which is very close to the Perecquian project and to my own way of thinking. However, Klevan is relying almost solely on Stanley Cavell's[23] take on the everyday – or rather the 'ordinary' as Cavell refers to it (1994) – while Lefebvre does not get a mention.[24] In his conclusion, Klevan recognizes that while film is a suitable medium for revealing uneventful activities, those can be few and far between, even in undramatic movies. Having studied some of the key proponents of the everyday, Rohmer and Ozu amongst others, he concedes that their films invariably contain dramatic events, which, while playing a role, do not derail the overarching quotidian narrative stance. Klevan further posits that film's 'melodramatic tendencies are closely related to a flight from the everyday and ordinary' – a conundrum that Lawry sums up as follows: 'The movies are "onto something" too. They understand that what is needed is a heightened sense of reality which can overcome the everydayness [...] But the non-everydayness of the movies must somehow resemble the everydayness of ordinary life too' (Lawry, 1980, pp.554–555).

Realism, everyday life, the ordinary – and film

Klevan rightly noted that 'in ordinary language we are all prone to slippage, confusing aspects of realism(s) with the everyday' (Klevan, 1996, p.47). On the other hand, Lefebvre asks

> What does the word 'real' mean today? It is the given, the sensible and practical, the actual, the perceptible surface. As for daily life, the general opinion is that it forms part of reality. But does it coincide with it? No, for it contains something more, something less, and something else: lived experience, fleeting subjectivity – emotions, affects, habits, and forms of behaviour.
>
> *(Lefebvre, 2014, p.681)*

He makes the point that everyday life 'forms part of reality', implying that reality is larger than daily life. Indeed we can construe reality as encompassing the humdrum, the banal, the ordinary but also the exceptional – and much more. But for Lefebvre the key difference is the 'subjective' part of everyday life, in other words the 'human' dimension in all its emotional states, the affect, which comes on top of – or is part of – the mechanical unravelling of the daily routine. It differs from the 'real' that encompasses a much broader ensemble – of which everyday environment and architecture are part. That broader reality is objective and factual, and it does not involve affects or emotions. Buildings and streets don't have feelings, while users do. However, we must complement and extend Lefebvre's attempt at defining everyday life in relation to reality. Lefebvre is correct to point out that the two overlap but do not coincide. But we also need to differentiate between the everyday and the ordinary and consider the following distinction proposed by Lorraine Sim:

> While the 'everyday' is the term most commonly employed in cultural studies and cultural theory at the present time, [Virginia] Woolf uses the word 'ordinary' with much more frequency [...] Furthermore, while the everyday in cultural studies tends to centre upon the sphere of human activities – particularly patterns of work, leisure and consumption – Woolf's preoccupation with the ordinary signals her keen interest in things (material objects both natural and human-made), in addition to daily experiences and behaviours. Also, the everyday implies a degree of repetition and, potentially, monotony which is not an implicit aspect of the ordinary. Something can be ordinary without being everyday. For example, illness, celebrations and falling in love are a part of ordinary experience and life but are not typically a part of everybody's everyday life. Such subtle differences between the terms 'everyday' and 'ordinary' are important ones, and because of this the two are not viewed as synonymous, although they do, of course, overlap in many ways.
>
> *(Sim, 2013, pp.2–3)*

Sim, in my opinion, accurately differentiates between the ordinary and the everyday, in the sense that they are not synonymous, although they are very close concepts. They are synonymous in terms of our everyday vocabulary, but need to be differentiated when it comes to everyday life studies. As noted previously, Cavell almost invariably uses the term 'ordinary' – while

Lefebvre, Perec and de Certeau do not appear to make a distinction. It may prove useful to differentiate between the two, especially when it comes to material things, such as objects in the home, furniture etc., as part of the 'ordinary', as well as 'ordinary events' that do not necessarily occur on a daily basis. 'Ordinary' – as in the *as found* concept – was also the term used by Alison and Peter Smithson[25] (see previous section).

When it comes to film, however, Torben Grodal makes the following point regarding the everyday and realism:

> Historically, realism has been associated with the representation of scenes from everyday life, especially the life of the middle and lower classes. Thus many critics regard De Sica's *Bicycle Thieves* as the prototypical realist film because it portrays everyday problems encountered by ordinary working-class people. Clearly, brushing your teeth is a more ordinary and therefore a more typical event than having a heart attack, winning a million dollars, or being raped. However, confining realism to the depiction only of the most statistically common actions would go counter to the general understanding of the concept among both viewers and critics. Thus, scenes of intense activity in critical situations, such as an emergency room or a workers' strike – as, for example, in Biberman's *Salt of the Earth* – may be perceived as realistic.
>
> *(Grodal, 2009, p.257)*

Grodal here makes a very useful point that helps us to hone in further on defining and distinguishing between the everyday, the ordinary and realism in film. He rightly puts forward the idea that restricting realism to the everyday is not a viable concept. In that sense he agrees with Lefebvre's idea that the two notions overlap but do not coincide. Indeed there are films or film scenes that might be considered realistic – say, for example, the battle scenes in Spielberg's *Saving Private Ryan* (1998) – but they can't be construed as part of everyday life. Neither are they ordinary. They are to be considered as exceptional, and belong to the 'once in a lifetime' type of situation. They go well beyond the ordinary disruption of the everyday. On the other hand, for example Noriko's wedding in Ozu's *Late Spring* (1949) or the act of selling the house in Hogg's *Exhibition* (2013) are both part of ordinary life – admittedly they are major events but well within the norm of ordinary lives, and eventually get absorbed by the relentlessness of everyday life. I am mainly interested in considering films that are within the range of the everyday and the ordinary – although the exceptional may also occasionally contain some useful nugget. However, in order to understand the mechanisms related to the cinematic everyday life and the ordinary, we must also consider how it can be revealed through disruptions, the subject of the next section.

Notes

1 An interesting discussion on the overlaps and differences between Rouch & Morin with Vertov's approach can be found in McDonough, 2007, p.12 – also McDonough highlights key divergences between Debord and Rouch & Morin's approach – see pp.17–18.

2 He further argues that this operates 'at the level of énonciation' whereby 'the enunciative situation created by the "crossing" of genres and media reflects a fusion of theory and practice that demonstrate how change is not simply an objective fact but above all something that is lived through, in a continuous process of alienation and appropriation' (Sheringham, 2006, p.334).

3 Avant-garde film-maker Jonas Mekas, commenting on his approach to his *365-day Project*, goes on to say '...during the *365 Day Project*, I became interested in how to eliminate that transformation. The challenge is how to record moments of real life and catch the essence of the moment in one unbroken take. No editing. One take, one shot. It sounds easy, but it's not. You have to be able to wait patiently for that moment. I continue to face the most difficult challenge: being really individual while taping real life situations. I think I am coming closer to succeeding, but it takes a total submersion of my own identity; it's a meeting of trance and madness'.

4 Realism in real life is just as complex and the whole notion of what's real or not has occupied philosophers of mind for some time – see, for example, Sellars' well known example of the coloured tie argument, where a tie may appear blue inside a shop under electric light but green in daylight (Sellars, 1997, pp.142–143). It also links to the issue of points of view in film – as well as real life. Take, for example, Tarantino's *Jackie Brown* (1997), the scene in the mall where Max and Melanie observe Jackie just before picking up the bag in the changing booth – the same scene is played twice – from Jackie's point of view and then from Max and Melanie's. And both times we may notice different things...which one is real?

5 When Lefebvre wrote those lines in 1958, it was a time when *La Nouvelle Vague* was about to erupt and he was most likely referring here to Hollywood movies of the 1950s shot in the studio with lavish sets and costumes, as well as French films of the so-called *qualité française* that was fiercely criticized by Truffaut and others for being essentially mediocre and unambitious.

6 For Lefebvre, Brecht's theatre has 'magnificently understood the epic content of everyday life' [*Brecht a magnifiquement discerné le contenu épique de la vie quotidienne*] (Lefebvre, 1958, p.27).

7 Le monde bourgeois, aussi nécessairement qu'il produit des machines et des hommes-machines, produit l'homme aberrant. Il produit le Vagabond, *son image inverse* (Lefebvre, 1958, p.18).

8 Lefebvre articulates this idea at some length: 'Here for the first time we encounter a complex problem, both aesthetic and ethical, that of the *reverse image*: an image of everyday reality, taken in its totality or as a fragment, reflecting that reality in all its depth through people, ideas and things which are apparently quite different from everyday experience, and therefore exceptional, deviant, abnormal [...] Chaplin gave us a genuine reverse image of modern times: its image seen through a living man, through his sufferings, his tribulations, his victories. We are now entering the vast domain of the illusory reverse image. What we find is a false world: firstly because it is not a world, and because it presents itself as true, and because it mimics real life closely in order to replace the real by its opposite; by replacing real unhappiness by fictions of happiness, for example – by offering a fiction in response to the real need for happiness – and so on. This is the 'world' of most films, most of the press, the theatre, the music hall: of a large sector of leisure activities. How strange the split between the real world and its reverse image is' (Lefebvre, 2014, p.34).

9 'Marxist playwright Bertold Brecht called for a rejection of realism in favour of texts that employed distanciation. According to the Brechtian view, it is only via this active refusal of realism, or anti-realism (as seen, for example, in some avant-garde film, countercinema, and Third Cinema), that the dialectical complexity of the world could be properly apprehended' (Kuhn and Westwell, 2012).

10 'Brecht breaks with the theatre of illusions as it does with the (Naturalist) theatre which imitates life. It does not purify the everyday; and yet it clarifies its contradictions. In its own way, it filters it. It

48 Everydayness and cinema

throws its weak part away: the magical part. Thus the Brechtian dramatic image differs from what we called the reverse image in Chaplin. Brecht aims (and he has said so) at an image which will master the facts' (Lefebvre, 2014, p.45).

11 Overall very few films appear to find Lefebvre's favour and he mentions only a handful throughout the three volumes but, for example, speaks enthusiastically of Karel Reisz's *Saturday Night and Sunday Morning* (1960) in relation to the ordinary life of young factory workers – to which he refers to (in a footnote) as 'an excellent film' (Lefebvre, 2014, p.869).

12 'Trop souvent, les écrivains, auteurs ou metteurs en scène « réalistes» accomplissent l'opération contraire. Au lieu de dégager l'extraordinaire de l'ordinaire, ils prennent l'ordinaire comme tel (les actes moyens d'un homme comme les autres, les événements moyens d'un jour comme les autres) et ils s'efforcent maladroitement de les rendre intéressants en les "montant en épingle", en les grossissant : en déclarant qu'ils sont très intéressants. Alors qu'ils ont seulement bariolé de couleurs fausses la grisaille de la vie prolétarienne, paysanne ou petite-bourgeoise. Comme le disait Brecht, ces « réalistes» répètent obstinément que la pluie tombe de haut en bas' (Lefebvre, 1958, p.21).

13 'Le plus extraordinaire, c'est aussi le plus quotidien ; le plus étrange, c'est souvent le plus banal, et la notion de « mythique », aujourd'hui, transcrit illusoirement cette constatation. Dégagé de son contexte, c'est-à-dire de ses interprétations, et de ce qui l'aggrave mais aussi le rend supportable – présenté dans sa banalité, c'est-à-dire dans ce qui le fait banal, étouffant, accablant – le banal devient l'extraordinaire et l'habituel devient "mythique". De même, une humble plante dégagée de la terre et des autres herbes, vue de près, devient une merveille. Mais alors il devient très difficile d'enchaîner de telles images, d'abord dégagées de leur contexte quotidien, pour les présenter dans leur quotidienneté essentielle. C'est le secret du talent de Fellini (*La Strada*) ou des réalisateurs du *Sel de la terre*, et c'est la (peut-être) une possibilité du réalisme' (Lefebvre, 1958, pp.20,21).

14 I have assumed here that it is Biberman's *Salt of the Earth* that Lefebvre refers to, although he doesn't mention either the director or the year.

15 '80% des éléments et des objects qui nous aident à vivre ne sont qu'aperçus par nous dans la vie courante, tandis que 20% sont vus. J'en déduis que le cinématographe fait cette révolution de nous faire voir tout ce qui n'a été qu'aperçu. Le chien qui passe dans la rue n'est qu'entrevu. Projeté à l'écran il est vu et tellement que toute la salle réagit comme si elle découvrait le chien. Le seul fait de projeter l'image qualifie déjà l'objet, il devient spectacle. Une image judicieusement cadrée vaut déjà par ce fait. Ne quittez pas ce point de vue. Là est le pivot, la base de ce nouvel art' (Léger, 1922).

16 Interestingly Lefebvre refers to this well known statement at the same time as Husserl's comment on the 'formlessness of the lived' in Volume 2 under 'the theory of moments' section (Lefebvre, 2014, p.650).

17 For more on cinephilia, see Keathley's book on the subject (Keathley, 2006) and as an example, we can refer to the scene when Amélie, in *Amélie* (Jeunet, 2001), is at the movies and spots a fly on the screen in *Jules et Jim* (Truffaut, 1962).

18 The concept of familiarity is briefly evoked by Lefebvre, who sees it as a *masque de connaissance* that veils the everyday reality – the Hegelian concept of 'What is familiar is not understood precisely because it is familiar' (Lefebvre, 1958, p.22).

19 As Adorno doesn't give any film example, we have to turn to Paula Amad who cites the Albert Kahn archive as an example of radical naturalism, venturing that 'the entire Kahn project inherited the excessive traits of Zola's literary naturalism, while also magnifying them because of the even more wayward filmic contingencies of what Theodor Adorno called, in reference to the medium's Zola-esque potential, an aesthetic of "radical naturalism" [...] the stubbornly unedited Kahn footage tipped the balance in their films away from narrative order to descriptive disorder' (Amad, 2010, p.95). Amad's book presents an excellent analysis of the Albert Kahn archive, where the everyday in early cinema is thoroughly investigated, in particular through the writings of Bergson, Kracauer and many others. Albert Kahn founded *Les Archives de la Planète* and from 1908 until 1931 his cameramen collected moving images from forty-eight countries across the globe.

20 'Narration establishes proportions', Lukács maintained, 'description merely levels'. Where there is proportion — one person understood in relation to another, person and environment conceived as foreground and background — there can be meaning. Where there is meaning, there can be value (moral, social, political). All these things Lukács found in Walter Scott and Balzac. Description, by contrast, merely levels. 'It accumulates useless and more often than not inelegant detail. It omits to sort the significant from the insignificant. It declassifies' (Trotter, 2008, p.152).

21 Trotter further defines literary naturalism as follows: 'Naturalist fiction envisaged instead a rapid physical rise to the moment of reproduction in the twenties, then a long redundancy accelerated by the emergence of some innate physical or moral flaw. What is left, after reproduction, and sometimes as a result of reproduction, is waste. In his Rougon-Macquart novels (1871–93), which describe the effects of heredity and environment on the members of a single family, tracing the passage of a genetic flaw down the legitimate line of the Rougons and the illegitimate line of the Macquarts, Emile Zola figured this long redundancy as a gradual, horrifying extrusion of dirt and disorder' (Trotter, 2008, p.150). Trotter further gives another account of what is a naturalist film by using a fiction film example: '*Ratcatcher* is a Naturalist film. The dustmen's strike has turned the housing estate into a "place of deterioration", as Ramsay puts it. James's destiny is "written", she notes, in the harshness of his surroundings. Zola himself could not have made it clearer that there is no hope for this young boy immured in dirt and disorder. The heuristic advantage of determinism (a far greater one than historians of either literature or film have been prepared to acknowledge) is that it opens up the chain of causes and effects to minute inspection. We know roughly what is going to happen, and can concentrate instead on the how and why. How is it, exactly, that one thing leads to another, and why?' (Trotter, 2008, p.151).

22 Klevan's book is to my knowledge the only scholarly work devoted to the subject of fiction films and everyday life.

23 As a philosopher Cavell has written at length on film – see for example Cavell, 1981 and Cavell, 1979. Scepticism is central to his take on cinema – see for example two films of the comedies of remarriage genre – *The Awful Truth* (Leo McCarey, 1937) and the melodrama of the unknown woman, *Blonde Venus* (Josef von Sternberg, 1932).

24 De Certeau is briefly mentioned in a footnote.

25 It might also be tempting to speculate that the term 'ordinary' is particularly used in England and stands for the everyday.

References

Adorno, T. W. (2005) *Minima Moralia : Reflections on a Damaged Life / Theodor Adorno*. Translated from the German by E. F. N. Jephcott. Radical Thinkers. London: Verso.

Amad, P. (2010) *Counter-Archive: Film, the Everyday, and Albert Kahn's Archives de la Planète*. Film and Culture. New York: Columbia University Press.

Berke, D. and Harris, S. (1997) *Architecture of the Everyday*. 1st edition. Princeton Architectural Press.

Cavell, S. (1979) *The World Viewed: Reflections on the Ontology of Film*. Cambridge, Mass.; Harvard University Press.

Cavell, S. (1981) *Pursuits of Happiness: The Hollywood Comedy of Remarriage*. Cambridge, Mass.; Harvard University Press.

Cavell, S. (1994) *In Quest of the Ordinary: Lines of Skepticism and Romanticism / Stanley Cavell*. Chicago: University of Chicago Press.

Cavell, S. (2005) *Cities of Words: Pedagogical Letters on a Register of the Moral Life*. Harvard University Press.

Grodal, T. (2009) *Embodied Visions: Evolution, Emotion, Culture, and Film*. OUP USA.

Keathley, C. (2006) *Cinephilia and History, Or, The Wind in the Trees*. Bloomington, IN: Indiana University Press.

Keiller, P. (2013) *The View from the Train: Cities and Other Landscapes*. Verso.

Klevan, A. (1996) 'Disclosure of the Everyday: The Undramatic Achievements in Narrative Film'. PhD [Online] University of Warwick. http://wrap.warwick.ac.uk/4099/.

Kuhn, A. and Westwell, G. (2012) *A Dictionary of Film Studies*. 1st edn. Oxford University Press.

Lawry, E. G. (1980) 'Literature as Philosophy: "The Moviegoer"'. *The Monist* 63 (4): 547–557.

Lefebvre, H. (1958) *Critique de La Vie Quotidienne – Vol. 1 – Introduction*. [2e éd.]. Le 'Sens de La Marche.' Paris: L'Arche.

Lefebvre, H. (2014) *Critique of Everyday Life*. The three-volume text. London: Verso.

Léger, F. (1922) 'La Roue, Sa Valeur Plastique'. *Comoedia*.

Lukács, G. (1974). *Soul and Form*. London: Merlin.

Lynch, K. (1960) *The Image of the City*. MIT Press.

McDonough, T. (2007) 'Calling from the inside: Filmic Topologies of the Everyday'. *Grey Room*, 6–29.

Mekas, J. (2010) 'Brief Glimpses of Beauty'. In *Making Movies*, edited by Elena Ochoa Foster, 14–15. C International Photo Magazine 10. London: Actar.

Ross, K. (1996) *Fast Cars, Clean Bodies: Decolonization and the Reordering of French Culture*. MIT Press.

Sellars, W. (1997) *Empiricism and the Philosophy of Mind*. Cambridge, Mass.: Harvard University Press.

Sheringham, M. (2006) *Everyday Life: Theories and Practices from Surrealism to the Present*. Oxford: Oxford University Press.

Sim, L. (2013) *Virginia Woolf: The Patterns of Ordinary Experience*. Ashgate Publishing Ltd.

Slessor, C. (2015) 'AR Issues: Architects Don't Invent, They Transform'. *ArchDaily*. March 2. http://www.archdaily.com/604164/ar-issues-architects-don-t-invent-they-transform/.

Trotter, D. (2008) 'Lynne Ramsay's Ratcatcher: Towards a Theory of Haptic Narrative'. *Paragraph* 31 (2): 138–158.

Venturi, R., Scott Brown, D. and Izenour, S. (1972) *Learning from Las Vegas*. Cambridge, Mass.: MIT Press.

Whyte, W. H. (2001) *The Social Life of Small Urban Spaces*. New York: Project for Public Spaces Inc.

3

THE VALUE OF FICTION AND THE ROLE OF DISRUPTIONS

In order to understand today's world, we need cinema, literally. It's only in cinema that we get that crucial dimension we are not ready to confront in our reality. If you are looking for what is in reality more real than reality itself, look into the cinematic fiction.[1]

Slavoj Žižek (2006)[2]

How can we fail to believe in the marvellous, the strange, the bizarre, when there are people who lead marvellous (or seemingly marvellous) lives full of departures and incessant changes of scenery, lives which we see carefully reflected in the cinema and the theatre and novels?

Henri Lefebvre (2014, p.141)

This section builds from the previous section on realism and pertains to the discussion on the 'disruption of the everyday', the next section. It essentially charts some of the facets of the value of fiction films within the parameters of this research, and is by no means claiming to be exhaustive. In the process I attempt here to address some key questions to clarify the position as to the value of fiction films in relation to everyday life.

As discussed in the previous section, Klevan seems to mourn the fact that melodramatic events and actions are getting in the way of the uneventful films. Not so, I contend. Everyday life is the base from which events emerge – without it there would be nothing to disturb; likewise the everyday is enhanced and reinforced by exceptional events. There is indeed no point in stating time and again that *la pluie tombe de haut en bas*[3] [rain falls from the sky], there is no value in promoting an everyday that states the obvious. Lefebvre reminds us that exceptional activities always have to be verified and validated by the everyday life that measures and embodies the changes (Lefebvre, 2014, p.339). Likewise in film, everyday life needs the disturbance and vice-versa; they are two sides of the same coin, they feed from each other, authenticate one another and are enhanced by each other's presence.

But what type of films are suitable for the study of everyday life?[4] The everyday is present in all films, including the most action-packed. It is simply that the relative proportion of drama/action to everyday life may vary greatly from one film to another – between nothing happening and the high-octane car chase, there are many shades of grey in the chiaroscuro of the everyday. The 'everyday by stealth' is always there, lurking in the background. For example, in *The Godfather* (Francis Ford Coppola, 1972), not a film reputed for its ordinariness, there is an unexpected kitchen scene where Pete (Richard Castellano) teaches Michael (Al Pacino) how to make a pasta sauce.[5]

There are always loopholes for the everyday to emerge or re-emerge, for it is an irrepressible force. However tiny, such scenes plant the everyday seed in the mind of the spectator. It is the great leveller that allows the audience to find their bearings. It is 'the everyday by synecdoche' – a small part standing for a much larger whole. Even a small particle of 'everyday DNA' in a film is worth having and can help to reconstruct a much larger ensemble of everydays. Using a cognitivist approach, Carroll and Seeley suggest that the everyday routine is a way of explaining our 'natural' comprehension of movies – that our day-to-day activities involving a constant shifting of positions, moving around, create a cadence, a rhythm, not unlike the cuts at the movies.[6] They perceive movies just as we perceive ordinary events in everyday contexts. Rejecting both the illusion thesis – that film amounts to an illusion of reality – and the film language metaphor, they propose a brand of cognitivism that 'lies both between and outside film realism and the film language hypothesis' (Carroll and

FIGURE 3.1 The kitchen scene in *The Godfather* (Francis Ford Coppola, 1972)

Seeley, 2013, p.58), partly based on an everyday schema of visual routines.[7] But Grodal, also adopting a cognitivist approach, goes a step further by proclaiming that film 'does not possess a semblance of reality; it is not an illusion, as has been claimed by numerous scholars and film critics; on the contrary, *film is part of reality*' (Grodal, 1997, p.11),[8] a statement that is in line with Hochberg's own observation 'perceiving the world and perceiving pictures of it may not be all that different, once you grasp how to look and what to ignore' (Peterson et al., 2007, p.402). In other words, the value of studying everyday life in film is that it closely coincides with real-life situations, if only we know what to look for and what to ignore – and don't expect the two to coincide, as noted in the last chapter.

Films, especially films shot on location, provide a large amount of documentation, from daily life in streets and buildings to 'items so small they would be otherwise imperceptible' (Hughes, 1976, p.52), often recorded unwittingly. In that sense, film is 'overflowed by its contents […] we may call it "film museum", a museum of objects and gestures, of attitudes and social behaviour which often elude the intention of the director' (Ferro, 1976, p.81). But how do fiction films compare to documentaries? On this topic, Ferro states that

> the social reality contained in a fiction film is not of the same kind as that which is proffered by a piece of reporting, by newsreels. It needs to be observed that there are nevertheless areas of overlap between these two types of film […] certain films of Jean-Luc Godard, for instance *Deux ou trois choses que je sais d'elle*, are as much documentaries as works of fiction.[9]

Overlaps and differences between fiction films and documentaries have been explored at length by film-studies scholars and historians, and there is no need for me to dwell on them further. However, I postulate here that we must turn to fiction in order to study everyday life – films make us focus on a more approachable type of reality, lived situations. Film is a leveller of intellect and situations – it feeds our imagination with the sort of 'mental food' that we can easily assimilate. It facilitates the acquisition of previously unattainable knowledge and it promotes the cultivation of what we previously lacked. It expands our horizons, as suggested by Kracauer:

> Films tend to explore this texture of everyday life, whose composition varies according to place, people, and time. So they help us not only to appreciate our given material environment but to extend it in all directions. They virtually make the world our home.
>
> *(Kracauer, 1960, p.304)*

For example, much as I like Jonathan Meades' documentary on Brutalism (BBC4, 2014), a better introduction to the topic, and to a discussion, might be *A Clockwork Orange* (Stanley Kubrick, 1971) or *Fahrenheit 451* (François Truffaut, 1966). Both films are a form of everyday life practice of brutalism, while Meades simply talks about it, admittedly most eloquently. But the fiction 'does it' while the documentary 'shows it' – it is the difference between narration and description, between lived space and an account of space, between being in the space or standing outside it. When Hulot is in the Arpels' kitchen in *Mon Oncle* (1958), he does not talk to the camera, explaining how the modern kitchen works. No, he simply tries just about every possible utensil, for our enjoyment and with mixed results; in other words he 'practises' it and shows how the future might work out – or not, in this case.

Fiction and documentaries clearly complement each other, and one does not exclude the other. Let's take another example: *Home* (Ursula Meier, 2008) is a good introduction to a situation when a home is no longer a home because the environmental conditions have changed drastically, as the motorway in front of their house re-opens. It is a carefully observed situation from the point of view of Marthe (Isabelle Huppert), the mother, who hangs on to some sort of sanity through repetitive everyday practices in the face of the gradual erosion of the world around her. It is a form of ecocinema, addressing crucial issues of sustainability, pollution and changes in environmental conditions and how these affect a family in its daily routine.

Similarly, *Fish Tank* (Andrea Arnold, 2009) is the story of Mia (Katie Jarvis), a fifteen-year-old girl, a first-person point of view of illusions, aspirations, and nightmares in the classic vein of British social realism, shot on the Mardyke Estate (just across the Thames Estuary from

FIGURE 3.2 Hulot in *Mon Oncle* (Jacques Tati, 1958)

Dartford). It pretty much summarises all we would want to know about contemporary youth culture in the geographical area around the Thames Estuary…and not something that one would easily gather from sociological reports and government statistics.

Cinema, as a popular medium, also furnishes us with a keen reflection of popular attitudes,[10] often tackling complex issues. For example, *Amour* (Michael Haneke, 2012) confronts the theme of how to deal with the end of life, a touchy and topical societal theme given the increasingly ageing population. But how do we deal with this issue? How do architects know what it's like and what are the options and the implications? How do we start researching such complex topics?

Turning to *The Shining* (Stanley Kubrick, 1980), everything is familiar to start with – but as we know the everyday is the perfect cover for the germination of the uncanny.[11] Uncanny familiar figures gradually return from repression, and Jack's repressed violence and alcoholism are finally rising to the surface in the most disturbing way. Pallasmaa reminds us that 'Suppressed emotions, however, seek their object and exposure. Anxiety and alienation, hardly hidden by surface rationalization, are often the emotional contents of today's everyday settings'. The dimension of the *heimlich* hides its opposite, the *unheimlich*, always ready to enter the scene. Pallasmaa goes on,

> Even real architecture is an exchange of experiential feelings and meanings between the space constructed of matter and the mental space of the subject. It is evident that the art of cinema can sensitize the architectural profession itself for the subtleties of this interaction. The architecture of cinema utilizes the entire range of emotions, and the touching architecture of Tarkovsky's films, for instance, should encourage architects to expand the emotional contents of their spaces, designed to be actually dwelled and lived in. Construction in our time has normalized emotions into the service of the social situations of life and has, at the same time, censored the extremes of the scale of human emotions: darkness and fear, dreams and reverie, elation and ecstasy.
>
> *(Pallasmaa, 2007, p.35)*

Being able to 'experience' vicariously a full range of emotions is one of the benefits of fiction films, says Pallasmaa, in order to deconstruct the current normalizations of emotions and feelings.

Films can be construed as a form of 'equipment for living' (Young, 2000). They provide an accelerated education in lived and practised situations – film simplifies complex realities and makes them more accessible. They are not, and neither do we want them to be, objective representations of reality. Paraphrasing Raban, I consider the 'soft' film world of illusion, myth, aspiration, and nightmare to be as real, maybe more real, than the 'hard' one located on maps, in statistics, in monographs on urban sociology and demography and architecture (Raban, 1974, p.10). Ferro also remarks that a fiction film is often dismissed because it 'dispenses only a dream, as if the dream formed no part of reality, as though the imaginary were not one of the driving forces of human activity' (Ferro, 1976, p.81). Indeed, the poetic and soft side of film is a crucial complement to 'reality', whatever this might be.

The everyday in film and its disruption

What is drama after all, but life with the dull bits cut out.

Alfred Hitchcock (Truffaut et al., 1986, p.103)

Hitchcock's explanation of how suspense functions throws some light on the balance between drama and the everyday.[12] Essentially, Hitchcock makes the point that ordinary situations are the necessary foundations from which to build up suspense. The story of the bomb is being told against a background of trivial conversation between two characters, and Hitchcock needs those fifteen minutes of everydayness as a contrast to the drama ahead. Suspense is of course a particular type of situation, but I postulate here that we need to disrupt the everyday, and not necessarily with a bomb, in order to notice it. Films tend to present a routine by establishing some parameters, gradually building a world that then gets disturbed so that we can detect the difference from the everyday – or rather, from the film-maker's point of view, that dramatic events are staged in contrast to a 'baseline'.[13] The idea of disruption is of course central to the classical Aristotelian five-stage narrative arc[14] and has been part of cinema since its inception. We only have to refer to *L'Arroseur Arosé* (Louis Lumière, 1895) – the moment when the young boy mischievously steps on the watering hose constitutes the first cinematic disruption of a plot equilibrium. It is this contrast that keeps the spectators interested in the unfolding narrative on the screen, and it has been shown that high-octane films with no respite from constant action tend to be less effective at emotionally engaging the viewers.[15] A similar point was made by Cavell regarding literature:

A familiar form of narrative opens by laying out a time and place in which a character or characters in whom we are to take an interest are described as carrying on a way of life, and then the plot proper, as it were, begins with an element of change or interruption breaking into this world. An obvious instance is Jane Austen's *Pride and Prejudice*, where the interruption of the ordinary days of this little world is the unheralded appearance in it of a pair of rich and handsome bachelors.

(Cavell, 2005, p.8)

In *La Piscine* (Deray, 1969) we can observe different degrees of interruption of the everyday. The opening image shows the credits gently rolling over the shimmering swimming pool water, to reveal an idle Jean-Paul (Alain Delon) lying by the side of the pool. The camera glides over the pool to frame Jean-Paul finishing his drink while a distant voice calls him, though he does not answer. This initial shot lasts just under a minute and establishes an atmosphere pertaining to a holiday scene. After that, Jean-Paul's summer rêverie is disrupted by Marianne (Romy Schneider) diving into the pool and splashing him. Marianne splashing Jean-Paul is a form of disruption of an everyday routine – sunbathing in this case – but has no dramatic impact on the course of the film. It's a very minor blip on the everyday landscape. Following a similar

FIGURE 3.3 The moment of disruption in *La Piscine* (Jacques Deray, 1969)

pattern as in *Pride and Prejudice,* the real step change occurs when Harry (Maurice Ronet), Marianne's former lover, and his daughter Pénélope (Jane Birkin) drop in on them for a visit.

Harry and Pénélope's arrival breaks into Jean-Paul and Marianne's baseline routine. However, the change brought about by new arrivals is quickly absorbed and a new everydayness emerges as everybody settles into summer activities à quatre instead of à deux. The real dramatic change occurs when Jean-Paul drowns Harry. After that there is no more everyday – everything is different from the previous days – even the weather turns: it's the end of the summer and of the film. This briefly exemplifies what Lefebvre calls the 'double dimension of the everyday', which is made of 'platitude and profoundness, banality and drama. And yet it is in the everyday that human dramas ravel and unravel, or remain unravelled' (Lefebvre, 2014, p.359).

Most films start by establishing a baseline of everydayness, creating a climate and an atmosphere of ordinariness for viewers to ease themselves in. Let's consider the opening sequence of *Blue Velvet* (Lynch, 1986) where in ten montage-style shots, Lynch paints, at least on the surface, a portrait of ideal small-town America, but one that Kael identified as an uncanny form of everydayness

> three minutes into the film [...] you recognize that this peaceful, enchanted, white-picket-fence community, where the eighties look like the fifties, is the creepiest sleepy city you've

ever seen [...] you're seeing every detail of the architecture, the layout of homes...furnishings and potted plants, the women's dresses [...] meticulously bright and sharp-edged

and yet

It's so hyperfamiliar, it's scary.

(Kael, 1990, p.203)

Indeed the idyllic everyday of the first few shots is rapidly eroded, first by the showing of a gun on the television screen inside the house, followed by the man who is watering his garden having a stroke.

At that point the everyday, always rampant, takes over briefly again as a small dog and a toddler play with the running water hose while the man is unconscious on the ground: life goes on. The everyday is finally thoroughly shattered when the camera penetrates under the family lawn, revealing a world of creepy crawlies, announcing the dark underbelly of Lumberton. At that point the uncanny has taken over, we are entering 'the anarchy and the chiaroscuro of everyday life'. However fleetingly brief this opening shot is, it is crucial to the creation of Lynch's film world.[16]

But in cinema, as in real life, the everyday is not enough. Lefebvre was adamant that we couldn't consider the everyday simply as 'the petty side of life, its humble and sordid element [...] it would be easy to make a critique of it, but not very meaningful: it would revert to old-fashioned populism' (Lefebvre, 2014, pp.336–337). The value of film is that it contributes to highlighting the everyday by contrasting it with the extraordinary and the dramatic. We need to assess the extraordinary against the banality of Perec's *infra-ordinaire* or, as remarked by Lefebvre, 'When a feeling or a passion avoids being tried and tested by the everyday, it demonstrates ipso facto its inauthenticity' (Lefebvre, 2014, p.359).[17] Pure action films may

FIGURE 3.4 Disruption of the everyday in *Blue Velvet* (David Lynch, 1986)

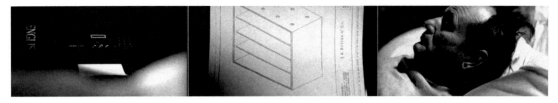

FIGURE 3.5 The intrusion of the fax in *Lost in Translation* (Sofia Coppola, 2003)

therefore lack in authenticity, as they need to be measured up against the everyday just as background needs foreground and vice-versa. And most film-makers follow this principle: even in films where one wouldn't expect it, there are moments of everydayness. For example in the scene of *Kill Bill 1* (Quentin Tarantino, 2003) when The Bride (Uma Thurman) visits the home of Vernita Green (Vivica A. Fox), one of the 'assassins' seeking revenge. As soon as she opens the door to her suburban home, a fierce battle ensues between the two rivals. Blood and sweat drip off their faces when a four-year-old girl appears carrying a lunch box: 'Mommy, I'm home!' The fight stops and the two women repair to the kitchen and proceed to have a cup of coffee while Vernita fixes some cereal for her daughter. But as she puts her hand in the 'Kaboom' cereal box, she fires a gun that shatters The Bride's coffee cup and she in return, throws a knife across the kitchen, killing Vernita. In this scene we have in quick succession the entrance [ordinariness], the fight [action], the little girl's entrance [ordinariness], the kitchen coffee and the cereal-fixing scene [ordinariness] followed by Vernita's killing [action]. Both moments of action and ordinariness are embroiled in a 'reactivated circuit' where they feed into each other. Ordinariness provides some form of respite and normality that allows the viewer to regroup and reconnect to a familiar sense of reality, making the ensuing actions all the more effective.

But there are of course much subtler forms of disruption of the everyday. Let's take for example the scene in *Lost in Translation* (Sofia Coppola, 2003) when jet-lagged Bob (Bill Murray), stranded in his hotel room in Tokyo and unable to sleep, receives a fax at 4:20am from his Californian wife, asking him to make decisions about the shelves in his study. The fax stuttering through is like a slice of everyday life being made visible as it blurts out of the fax machine…a rare case of an invasion of everydayness in the middle of an heterotopia.

There is also of course the amusing scene in *Amélie* (Jean-Pierre Jeunet, 2001), where Amélie has subtly altered some elements in Collignon's flat, as well as advancing the alarm clock to 4am. Getting up like a zombie, Collignon approaches the bathroom door but misses the knob, as it has been switched around, and nearly loses his balance as a result. This shows that subtle alterations to our everyday routine and environment can indeed be very disruptive – and is a neat example of muscle memory being tricked and how it is completely integrated in our everyday gestures.[18]

Another little-discussed form of disruption is boredom, as identified by Blanchot: 'Boredom, is the everyday becoming visible – or rising to the surface – having therefore lost its primary trait – that of being overlooked' (Blanchot, 1969, p.361).[19] Of course, in the everyday, the

FIGURE 3.6 Parallel universes in *Stunned Man* (Julian Rosefeldt, 2004)

repetitive nature of the same actions may induce boredom, which might in turn lead to more disruption. This is amply visible in Julian Rosefeld's *Stunned Man* (2004), a film shot on two screens side-by-side with mirrored flats on each side. The same actor in each flat goes about his everyday activities in exactly the same way, but not at the same time. It exposes the routines, stereotypes, and absurdities of everyday life in minute detail over 32 minutes. It is shot in real time, with a very mobile camera following the actors. Ordinary routines are painstakingly observed: making coffee, working at a computer screen, reading the papers, checking the fridge, tidying up, going to the bathroom etc. The characters are pretty restless and do not settle on a task for a long time. But at some point the character on the right kicks his bookshelf, which collapses. Unperturbed, he carries on preparing a bowl of noodles but drops it on the floor. He starts to clean up with a broom, but rapidly uses the broomstick as a weapon, and in a display of martial art-cum-slapstick, he destroys just about everything in the flat, the equivalent of a domestic road rage. Later he settles and gradually puts things back in order, while the character on the left, having by that time also dropped his bowl of noodles, proceeds to systematically trash his flat in a similar fashion. It is a case of boredom having risen to the surface and acting as a disturbance of the everyday life routine…and crucially we can witness it building up in real time. As for the dropping of the bowl, it is a classic form of domestic accident acting as a disturbance. And the destruction of the flat, followed by the tidying-up phase, exposes the various mechanisms of disruptions of the everyday up to the point where it eventually gets re-established and the equilibrium is restored, and in the process it also highlights the link between entropy and the everyday.[20] *Stunned Man* is an exemplary film to demonstrate the concept, especially as disruption and everydayness are eerily displayed asynchronously side-by-side over the two screens.

Indeed, we need this repetitive reactivation between both states in order to be able to taste the difference. This necessity is, in effect, what we rely on to uncover the everyday in film. If it was all action, there would be no quotidian for us to study – the extraordinary 'only makes sense when its brilliance lights up the sad hinterland of everyday dullness' (Lefebvre, 2014, p.650) and the corollary is also true: if it was all about the quotidian, the everyday would be reduced to 'empty moments [...] unable to grasp the exciting risks moments propose' (Lefebvre, 2014, p.650). We need to grasp the extraordinary that shines through the ordinary, the extra-quotidian that breaks up daily life as well as appreciating the hidden layers of infra-ordinary that colonize popular culture. We have to learn to tease out such precious moments – almost as if taking advantage of moments when film-makers are off-guard. In just about every movie, such nuggets are there for the picking.

Notes

1 Žižek adds: 'Our fundamental delusion today is not to believe in what is only a fiction, to take fictions too seriously. It's, on the contrary, not to take fictions seriously enough. You think it's just a game? It's reality. It's more real than it appears to you [...] Cinema is the art of appearances, it tells us something about reality itself. It tells us something about how reality constitutes itself'.

2 *The pervert's guide to cinema by Slavoj Žižek* (Sophie Fiennes, 2006).

3 Lefebvre quoting Brecht – see previous chapter.

4 Regarding the type of everyday films, Grodal argues that 'Representations of the private lives of film stars or millionaires may be just as realistic as "kitchen sink" representations of the lives of ordinary people, but the latter will often be considered more typical and therefore more realistic than the former' (Grodal, 2009, p.252).

5 Pete, addressing Michael: 'come over here, kid, learn something, you never know, you might have to cook for 20 guys someday. You see, you start out with a little bit of oil...then you fry some garlic... then you throw in some tomatoes, tomato paste, you fry it...ya make sure it doesn't stick...you get it to a boil...you shove in all your sausage and your meatballs...and a little bit of wine...and a little bit of sugar...that's my trick'...at which point Sonny (James Caan) interrupts 'why don't you cut the crap...how's Paulie?' to which Pete answers 'you won't see him no more', the reason being that Paulie had been gunned down by Pete and an accomplice in the preceding scene. Sonny's interruption signals the end of that particular everyday moment and the return to action.

6 'The shot/sequence structure of scenes [...] stand-in for the visual routines that keep our attention fixed to diagnostic features in ordinary contexts – they map to the visual routines that would putatively govern our patterns of attention if we were present in the depicted actions. The frequency of such scenes helps explain the widespread accessibility of movies as well as why they feel so real – sequences constructed on the interested observer mimic the structure and cadence of those patterns of attention constitutive of the everyday perceptual experiences that they depict' (Carroll and Seeley, 2013, p.66).

7 'The use of variable framing within many (but scarcely all) cinematic sequences approximates the structure and pacing of the visual routines that govern perception in everyday behavior [...] in the ordinary context of everyday activities we do not scan the environment searching for what we need [...] However, the bulk of each day is taken up with commonplace activities like dialing a telephone, operating machinery, writing at a desk, or getting lunch at the cafeteria. A significant proportion of the rest of what we do involves smooth coping with the environment, which involves the same kinds of stereotyped behaviors (e.g., turning door knobs, navigating hallways, and sitting down or getting up from desks or workstations). This entails that the cadence of ordinary conscious experience is, by and large, dictated by the cadence of those patterns of attention associated with those visual routines that govern these everyday activities. Likewise, the camera typically doesn't smoothly track actors or actions across the global development of a cinematic sequence. It jumps from one salient feature to the next, mimicking visual routines, building up the content of the depicted action or event out of a set of associated shots' (Carroll and Seeley, 2013, p.64).

8 Grodal explains further 'Mark Johnson (1987) has clearly shown the way in which images directly serve as the basis for establishing a cognitive relation between man and the world. The images are not

something else, but a kind of software which establishes and grounds our knowledge in the world [...] From this point of view, narrative structures or schemata are not in principle imposed from without, for instance on images, emotions or memories, but are related to the synthetic–functional processes by which our different mental faculties and different aspects of the world are connected. [...] Imagination, consisting of hypothetical simulations of possible relations and processes, is a central aspect of everyday life; the difference between art and everyday imagination is not of kind but of degree, of direct 'interestedness', and of 'art' understood as superior know-how (Grodal, 1997, p.11).

9 On the topic of *Deux ou trois choses que je sais d'elle* (1967), Godard concurs with Ferro: 'It is not a story, but hopefully a document to a degree where I think Paul Delouvrier himself should have commissioned the film. Actually, if I have a secret ambition, it is to be put in charge of the French newsreel services. All my films have been reports on the state of the nation; they are newsreel documents, treated in a personal manner perhaps, but in terms of contemporary actuality' (Godard, 1972, p.239).

10 On the issue regarding whether film is a good indicator of popular culture, Hughes argues that 'Though this commercialised self-consciousness deprives films of the innocent or naive spontaneity of folk culture, it does not render film unacceptable as a source for popular attitudes [...] Our concern as historians using film sources should be whether these hypotheses about popular attitudes are accurate ones. One of the virtues of this particular source is that the public's choices at the box-office provide a crude measure of the accuracy of film-makers' hypotheses about popular values [...] A film which accurately reflects their attitudes can fail (perhaps because of poor advertising and distribution, poor plot, bad casting, even general economic conditions), but a film which does not share some of the audience's fundamental orientations will not often succeed. In using feature films to gauge popular attitudes there is some basis, then, for working with successful films, particularly genre films. In addition, it is best to base our estimates of popular attitudes on a wide sample of films from a given period. As a check on the accuracy of our findings we can compare the results of our film analyses with studies of popular attitudes reflected in other forms of popular culture from the same period, and we can relate our findings to contemporaneous sociological studies of norms and values. For example, the vast literature on the nature and evolution of the American national character provides an extensive and intensive charting of American values over an extended period of time, against which we can compare the values and attitudes we detect in popular American films' (Hughes, 1976, pp.70–71).

11 'In his essay on the uncanny, *Das Unheimliche*, Freud said that the uncanny is the only feeling which is more powerfully experienced in art than in life. If the genre required any justification, I should think this alone would serve as its credentials', Stanley Kubrick (Pereira et al., 2013, p.252).

12 'Let's suppose that there is a bomb underneath this table between us. Nothing happens, and then all of a sudden, "Boom!" There is an explosion. The public is surprised, but prior to this surprise, it has seen an absolutely ordinary scene, of no special consequence. Now, let us take a suspense situation. The bomb is underneath the table and the public knows it, probably because they have seen the anarchist place it there. The public is aware the bomb is going to explode at one o'clock and there is a clock in the decor. The public can see that it is a quarter to one. In these conditions, the same innocuous conversation becomes fascinating because the public is participating in the scene. The audience is longing to warn the characters on the screen: "You shouldn't be talking about such trivial matters. There is a bomb beneath you and it is about to explode!" In the first case we have given the public fifteen seconds of surprise at the moment of the explosion. In the second case we have provided them with fifteen minutes of suspense. The conclusion is that whenever possible the public must be informed' (Truffaut et al., 1986, p.73).

13 The term 'baseline' is borrowed from my environmental and thermal modelling past, where an average baseline was needed in order to measure up variations from it. For example, we would refer to a typical year of weather data (Kew 1967 is often chosen, or at least was at the time). See Penz, 1983, p.319.

The value of fiction and the role of disruptions **63**

14 This is summarized by Maureen Thomas as follows: 'Tzvetan Todorov argues that narrative in its most basic form is a causal transformation of a situation through five stages:
- a state of equilibrium at the outset
- a disruption of the equilibrium by some action
- a recognition that there has been a disruption
- an attempt to repair the disruption
- a reinstatement of the initial equilibrium.

These changes of state are not random but are produced according to principles of cause and effect (e.g. principles that describe possibility, probability, impossibility, and necessity among the actions that occur) [...] this emergent form, or transformation, is a necessary feature of narrative [...]' (Thomas, 2012, p.287).

15 See More4 TV programme: 'What makes a masterpiece? Stories and Film', 2012.

16 'All my movies are about strange worlds that you can't go into unless you build them and film them. That's what's so important about film to me. I just like going into strange worlds. To give a sense of place, to me, is a thrilling thing. And a sense of place is made up of details. And so the details are incredibly important. If they're wrong, then it throws you out of the mood. And so the sound and music and color and shape and texture, if all those things are correct and a woman looks a certain way with a certain kind of light and says the right word, you are gone, you are in heaven. But it's all the little details' (http://www.thecityofabsurdity.com/quotecollection/place.html).

17 Adding 'Although the drama of love may well consist in it being "smashed against everyday life", in the words of Maiakovsky, the boat must brave the current or stay at its moorings' (Lefebvre, 2014, p.359).

18 Our spatial practices that we completely take for granted are shaped by the force of habit and our muscle memory, synonymous with motor learning. I was reminded of this by the conversation between two of my friends. C and D started a discussion on their everyday life and habits and C proceeded to explain how he prepares his slippers when going to bed, i.e by carefully placing them by the bed in such a way that, when waking up, he would sit on the edge of the bed, rotate and, without even opening his eyes, he would gently ease his still sleepy feet into the slippers...C told this story to D, mentioning that he had only found one other person who had the same routine...at which point D exclaimed, 'I do the same'. They nearly embraced – a real-life example that echoes the scene with Collignon.

19 My translation: 'L'ennui c'est le quotidien devenu manifeste : par conséquent ayant perdu son trait essential – constitutif – d'être *inaperçu*. Le quotidien nous renvoie donc toujours à cette part d'existence inapparente et cependant non caché, insignifiante parce que toujours en-deçà de ce qu'il signifie, silencieuse, mais d'un silence qui s'est déjà dissipé, lorsque nous nous taisons pour l'entendre et que nous écoutons mieux en bavardant, dans cette parole non parlante qui est le doux bruissement humain en nous, autour de nous' (Blanchot, 1969, p.361).

20 The second law of thermodynamics introduces the notion of entropy that can be equated to a measure of the disorder or messiness of a room that will only increase with time. In the case of *Stunned Man* we start with the equilibrium state – the everyday – that gets more and more disturbed by the destructive actions, towards a state of entropy, chaos.

References

Blanchot, M. (1969) *L'entretien infini*. Paris: Gallimard.
Carroll, N. and Seeley, W. P. (2013) 'Cognitivism, psychology, and neuroscience: movies as attentional engines in Psychocinematics', in Arthur P. Shimamura (ed.) *Psychocinematics: exploring cognition at the movies*. Oxford; New York: Oxford University Press. pp.53–75.

Cavell, S. (2005) *Cities of words: pedagogical letters on a register of the moral life*. Harvard University Press.

Ferro, M. (1976) 'The fiction film and historical analysis', in Paul Smith (ed.) *The Historian and Film*. Cambridge University Press.

Fiennes, S. (2006) *The pervert's guide to cinema by Slavoj Žižek*.

Godard, J.-L. (1972) *Godard on Godard: critical writings*. Cinema two series. Jean Narboni and Tom Milne (eds.). London: Secker and Warburg.

Grodal, T. (2009) *Embodied visions: evolution, emotion, culture, and film*. OUP USA.

Grodal, T. (1997) *Moving pictures: a new theory of film genres, feelings and cognition*. Oxford: Clarendon Press.

Hughes, W. (1976) 'The evaluation of film as evidence', in Paul Smith (ed.) *The Historian and Film*. Cambridge University Press.

Kael, P. (1990) *Hooked: film writings 1985–1988*. London: Boyars.

Kracauer, S. (1960) *Theory of film: the redemption of physical reality*. New York: Oxford University Press.

Lefebvre, H. (2014) *Critique of everyday life*. The three-volume text. London: Verso.

Pallasmaa, J. (2007) *The architecture of image: existential space in cinema*. Helsinki: Rakennustieto.

Penz, F. (1983) *Passive solar heating in the UK housing stock*. PhD thesis. University Library, University of Cambridge: University of Cambridge.

Pereira, B. J. G. et al. (2013) *Analyses of Cultural Productions: Papers of 30th Conference of Psyart Porto, 2013*. Porto: Lulu.com.

Peterson, M. A. et al. (2007) *In the mind's eye: Julian Hochberg on the perception of pictures, films, and the world*. OUP USA.

Raban, J. (1974) *Soft city*. London: Hamilton.

Thomas, M. (2012) 'The Moving Image of the City: Expressive Space/Inhabitation/ Narrativity: Intensive studio workshop on "Continuity of Action in space"', in François Penz and Andong Lu (eds.) *Urban Cinematics: Understanding Urban Phenomena Through the Moving Image*. Bristol; Chicago: Intellect. pp. 283–307.

Truffaut, F. et al. (1986) *Hitchcock*. New York: Simon & Schuster.

Young, S. D. (2000) Movies as equipment for living: a developmental analysis of the importance of film in everyday life. *Critical Studies in Media Communication*. 17 (4), 447–468.

4

GEORGES PEREC AND CHANTAL AKERMAN

Perec, *cinématographe* of the everyday

> *C'est une petite boîte noire. On met la pellicule à l'intérieur. On remonte le ressort, comme si c'était un réveille-matin. Au lieu de prendre une photographie, on va en prendre plusieurs à la suite, assez vite pour donner l'illusion du mouvement, de la vie. C'est ça le cinéma. C'est aussi simple que ça.* [It's a little black box. The film goes inside. We wind up the spring mechanism as if it were an alarm clock. Instead of taking one photograph, we'll take a few in quick succession to give the illusion of movement, of life. That's what cinema is about. It's as simple as that.]
>
> *Georges Perec* La Vie Filmée des Français *(de Bary, 2006, p.75)*

In Chapter 1 on Lefebvre and Perec, I examined Perec's role and link within the world of architecture. In this section I consider Perec the film-maker, and how his writing on the everyday translates into moving images. Perec is not widely known for his work with film, although he was actively involved in various roles. The filmography of Perec includes 13 titles (de Bary, 2006, pp.298–299), but the key films of relevance here are, in chronological order:

- *Un homme qui dort* (Bernard Queysanne and Perec, 1974), which is an adaptation from his novel of the same name published in 1967.[1]
- *La Vie Filmée des Français*, produced by Michel Pamart and Claude Ventura in 1975, for which he both wrote the commentary and read his text.
- *Les Lieux d'une Fugue* (Perec, 1978), the only film for which he is credited as the director. Produced by l'INA (Institut National de l'Audiovisuel).
- *Récits d'Ellis Island* (Bober and Perec, 1979), produced by l'INA.
- *Série noire* (Alain Corneau, 1979), a fiction film for which he was the scriptwriter.

66 Everydayness and cinema

Perec was also an occasional cinema critic and published some 20 articles in newspapers and journals between 1960 and 1981 (de Bary, 2006, pp.294–296). Moreover he collaborated, mainly as a scriptwriter, on 15 unfinished or unrealized film projects. Perec had therefore plenty of opportunities to engage with the moving image and reflect on how to work with the medium of film. He also went frequently to the cinema, and Eisenstein's *La Ligne Générale*[2] (1929) and Resnais's *Hiroshima Mon Amour* (1959) were lasting influences on him (Bellos, 1993, p.216).

We know from Perec's key manifesto *Approches de quoi* [Approaches to what] (Perec, 2008, p.209) – that the prime mode of investigation to interrogate *le banal, le quotidien, l'évident, le commun, l'ordinaire, l'infra-ordinaire, le bruit de fond, l'habituel* [the banal, the everyday, the obvious, the common, the ordinary, the infra-ordinary, the background noise, the usual] is description and enumeration: *Décrivez votre rue. Décrivez-en une autre [...] Questionnez vos petites cuillers. Qu'y a-t-il sous votre papier peint?* [Describe your street. Describe another [...] Interrogate your small spoons. What is underneath your wallpaper?]. He acknowledges the triviality of his interrogations that are barely indicative of a method, which is precisely what renders them all the more essential, given the failures of other investigations in search of grasping the truth[3] (*notre vérité*). But how did Perec *le cinématographe* use description and enumeration? How did they translate onto the screen and how effective was this form of interrogation in uncovering the quotidian? Some of Perec's most interesting texts on cinema can be found in *La Vie Filmée des Français*,[4] where he is commenting on early cinema images, silent amateur and actualité short films from 1930 to 1934:

> *Sur la femme à la passerelle* [About the woman on a footbridge]
>
> *C'est alors peut-être que se produit le miracle de l'image; sous la gaucherie du mouvement, sous l'imprécision de l'anecdote, quelque chose d'irremplaçable nous est restitué [...] l'attention portée à un être, à un événement dérisoire, à un geste oublié, à une quotidienneté enfouie sous les fracas de la grande Histoire, et qui resurgit soudain, intacte, merveilleuse* [It is perhaps at that moment that the miracle of the image takes place; despite the awkwardness of the movement and the imprecision of the anecdote, it restitutes something irreplaceable [...] the focus on a person, an anecdotal event, a forgotten gesture, a daily life buried under history with a capital H, and which suddenly reappears, intact, marvellous].
>
> *(de Bary, 2006, p.77)*

Perec reads in this short clip of a woman on a footbridge the miraculous reenactment of an everyday long buried under the weight of history – and with the passing years the celluloid becomes memory.

He goes on, commenting on a picnic scene by the sea as follows:

Sur le pique-nique [About the picnic]

On connaissait ce qui dure, ce dont on fait mémoire ou archives [...] Mais pas les gestes, pas ce temps intact immortalisé dans ce qu'il a de plus fluide, de plus inconsistant : ce qui n'aurait pas laissé de trace, ce dont on ne se saurait jamais souvenu : un homme qui se trémousse en imitant un chef d'orchestre ; une femme qui rectifie une mayonnaise ; deux hommes qui allument des cigarettes ; une journée à la mer, une belle journée où il a fait bien chaud [We knew what lasts, what becomes memory or archive [...] but not the gestures, not the untouched time immortalized in what is most fluid and inconsistent: what would have left no trace, which one would never remember: a man who wiggles while imitating an orchestra conductor; a woman who adjusts a mayonnaise; two men who light a cigarette; a day by the sea, a beautiful day when it was hot].

(de Bary, 2006, p.77)

In this scene, Perec's commentary is a list of disconnected micro-stories, the sum of its parts amounting to *une belle journée,* not just because of the weather, but a beautiful day in the sense of a perfect day that combines a nice warm day by the sea with gestures and scenes pertaining to the everyday but a particular type of everyday: leisure activities. And as we know from Lefebvre, leisure activities are an integral part of the everyday, together with work and family life, and where on holidays 'everyday life in its entirety becomes play' (Lefebvre, 2014, p.55). But there is no sense that Perec provided a critical comment on the everyday as leisure time.[5] Perec's description is characteristically neutral and factual – the enumeration is strangely disjointed[6] to the point where one isn't sure if the woman with the mayonnaise is in the same group as the two men with the cigarettes. It is a form of cinematic montage.

Looking back at the discussion on realism in Chapter 2, Perec's attitude to reality is obvious here, unsurprising since his entire project is steeped in realism.[7] Indeed, as James reminds us,

The term *infra-ordinaire* first appears in Perec's work in the 1970s. Perec's early writings on the novel insist instead on the notion of the 'real' and argue for a form of literary realism that leaves little room for chance. Echoing Lukacs's *Meaning of Contemporary Realism*, Perec argues in 'Pour une litterature réaliste' (1962; 'For a Realist Literature') that realism requires the selection of relevant details from the mass of inessential ones.

(James, 2009, p.193)

But we must now turn to cinema's influence on Perec's writing. In an interview regarding his script for *Série noire* (Alain Corneau, 1979), Perec recognizes the influence of cinema on his writing – he refers to the idea of tracking shots[8] in *La vie mode d'emploi* (Perec, 1978). At the same time Peytard coins the term écriture-cinéma.[9] If that is indeed the case, how does his écriture-cinéma translate onto the screen? Is Perec's writing already ready-made for film, as a

68 Everydayness and cinema

succession of shot lists? To understand how it works we must consider one of his films, *Un homme qui dort* (Bernard Queysanne and Perec, 1974).

Un homme qui dort

Un homme qui dort, produced in 1973, was a collaboration between Georges Perec and Bernard Queysanne. It is based on Perec's book of the same name, published in 1967 (Perec, 1967). The storyline is deceptively simple: a young man (Jacques Spiesser), the only character in the film, one day doesn't attend his exams and gradually falls into a state of indifference, cutting all links with society, friends and family alike. He spends most days and nights either sleeping or walking in the city. He lives in a tiny attic bedsit – *une chambre de bonne* – and goes through various stages of indifference over one year. At the end of the film he seems to be coming out of this state, and we have a sense that he might return to life.

It is partly autobiographical, something that happened to him in 1956, and he only wrote the book ten years later. And while he claimed that this was the most 'visual' of his books, he was well aware of the challenge of making a 'long métrage alors qu'il n'y a qu'un seul personnage, aucune histoire, aucune péripétie, aucun dialogue, mais seulement un texte lu par une voix-off' [a full-length fiction film with only one character, no storyline, no dialogue, only a voice-over] (Perec, 2007, p.44). The first challenge[10] he and Queysanne faced was to substantially cut the text, as it was far too long for a short film. The book alternates between action chapters and reflective chapters. The solution was to remove every other chapter, keeping only the action parts (Perec, 2007, p.47), and there was no rewrite from Perec.

The structure of the film is yet another attempt by Perec to work with an Oulipian constraint, the sestina.[11] Bellos records that,

> Unlike the novel, the film version of *Un homme qui dort* has a mathematical construction. After the prologue (part 0, so to speak) there are six sections, which Perec and Queysanne called, for ease of reference in the shooting and editing, l'apprentissage, le bonheur, l'inquiétude, les monstres, la destruction et le retour [Rupture, Apprenticeship, Happiness, Anguish, Monsters, and Return]. The six sections are interchangeable in the sense that the same objects, places, and movements are shown in each, but they are all filmed from different angles and edited in a different order, in line with the permutations of the sestina. The text and the music are similarly organised in six-part permutations, and then edited and mixed so that the words are out of phase with the image except at apparently random moments, the last of which – the closing sequence – is not random at all, but endowed with an overwhelming sense of necessity.
>
> *(Bellos, 1993, p.540)*

The six parts are also a departure from the book and they do not appear in the film as such; there are no headings. However, they are easily noticed by viewers, while the use of the sestina is pretty difficult to detect. It was probably very useful for Perec as a way of structuring the work, as part of the process, especially as it was his first film, and he would have been keen to hang on to a world of constraints as a means of providing some sort of guidance and rationality.

Everydayness

Un homme qui dort could be construed as a study of everydayness, of a particular type, that of a young man engaged in representative activities – or non-activities – although he might be living an atypical life. We are far from *métro-boulot-dodo*,[12] and yet there are useful moments that would be fairly universal and pertain to life in a tight space, a study in confined domesticity and how, on a daily basis, to live in a 'galetas long de deux mètres quatre vingt-douze, large d'un mètre soixante-treize, soit un tout petit peu plus de cinq mètres carrés' [a garret 2.92 metres long by 1.73 metres wide, so just over five square metres] (Perec, 2007, p.10).

Repeated gestures of everydayness are observed: plugging in the kettle, switching on the kettle, putting some Nescafé in a bowl, pouring the water into the bowl, drinking the coffee – on the bed, standing up or on the window ledge – recurrent shots of this type are observed throughout the film. Brushing his teeth, reading or not reading, washing his socks or observing his socks soaking in a plastic bowl, shaving at the basin. A particular representative sequence lasting over 90 seconds sees him entering the bedsit, making his bed, reading *Le Monde* on his bed, washing himself at the basin, preparing some toast, eating it on his windowsill and filling a bucket with water to wash some clothes.[13]

There is a whole panoply of movements and gestures on how to negotiate body postures on a small and narrow bed. We see him idling on his bed, smoking or just letting his gaze follow

FIGURE 4.1 *Un homme qui dort* (Bernard Queysanne, 1974): everyday life in a small place

a crack in the ceiling 'tu restes étendu sur ta banquette étroite, les bras derrière la nuque, les genoux haut' [you remain lying down on your narrow berth, arms behind your head, knees up] (Perec, 2007, p.9). This of course echoes Perec's own writing, in *Espèces d'espaces*, claiming his fondness for ceilings observed from his bed.[14]

There are long tracking shots where the camera eye lingers in close-up on shelves, on books, on objects on the shelves, on posters, on cracks in the door and on the basin tap. It is a tiny space and we could probably piece together every square inch of it gleaned across the film. Along the same lines Montfrans comments on the use of space by the character

> *qui construit et déconstruit son indifférence à partir des perceptions des objets qui l'entourent, obstinés dans leur nature d'objets, banaux, présents jusque dans ses expériences oniriques, d'abord rétifs, durs, indifférents, ensuite empreints d'angoisse'* [who constructs and deconstructs his indifference from the perception of objects around him, obstinate in their nature, ordinary objects, present even in his dreamlike experiences, at first reticent, hard, indifferent, then full of anguish].
>
> *(Montfrans, 1999, p.103)*

It is not only about the perception of objects but also their questioning, a very Perecquian concern, when he urges us to 'Questionnez vos petites cuillers. Qu'y a-t-il sous votre papier peint?', previously evoked.

At the level of the city there are also several moments of everydayness, especially in bars where the young man eats his regular steak frites, invariably seated on a high stool at the bar. There are at least three such scenes in the film, which could be read as a small ethnomethodological study in how to serve a client steak frites at a bar, with a glass of wine. Some of those scenes are relatively long and uninterrupted, with elements of continuity editing, as in the first one that lasts 1'10". Every time, the gestures are familiar and repetitive with only slight variations, in the space, in the shape of the glass, the type of stool, the people around. Similarly the film offers an intriguing array of scenes, showing him entering a cinema, putting out his cigarette and being shown to his seat by an usher with a torch. Some of those gestures, moments and practices have long gone, and this is where the film, unwittingly, also has an archival value.

But coming back to my original question, if it is indeed the case that we can detect in Perec an écriture-cinéma, how did it in turn translate onto the screen, and how effective was his approach in uncovering *le quotidien* through the medium of film? Perec's *le cinématographe* made full use of his formidable écriture-cinéma skills by using various techniques of description and enumeration as well as inventing numerous visual and other punning techniques. But above all he created and experimented with a new form of *cinema*-écriture, to uncover *l'endotique* and *l'infra-ordinaire* of *Un homme qui dort*. It is a unique experiment that reveals

FIGURE 4.2 *Un homme qui dort* (Bernard Queysanne, 1974): everyday scene in a Parisian bar

how his particular brand of *cinema*-écriture uncovered *le quotidien* of one man over one year, both in a domestic situation, in *la chambre de bonne*, as well as the day-to-day life of the city.

The case of Perec and Akerman

This section further elaborates on the use of film as a mode of investigation of the everyday, and for this purpose I am suggesting that several of Chantal Akerman's films have a similar interest to Perec's brand of everydayness and constitute a sort of parallel 'universe' to *Espèces d'espaces*. This is perhaps not surprising, given that Akerman's films are of the same period as Perec's writing, and the publication of *Espèces d'espaces* in 1974 pretty much coincides with Akerman's key film *Jeanne Dielman, 23 Quai du Commerce, 1080 Bruxelles* (*Jeanne Dielman* hereafter) in 1975. Both are key texts on the notion of the everyday, although *Jeanne Dielman* has usually been analysed for 'its thematic concern with women and the everyday [...] a reference in any discussion of feminist and women's film' (Margulies, 1996, pp.4–5).

To my knowledge, there is no evidence that Perec and Akerman either influenced or even knew each other, nor is there any comparative study of Perec and Akerman, scholarly or otherwise. As far as I am aware, they are never mentioned in the same breath – and yet they have a lot in common.[15] Moreover, Babette Mangolte, who was one of Perec's oldest and longest-lasting friends (Bellos, 1993, p.282), was director of photography on several of Akerman's films, including *Jeanne Dielman*.[16] There is therefore no doubt that they would have been aware of each other's existence through Mangolte. Akerman had much in common with Perec, aside from Mangolte, and in some ways she does with a camera what he does in writing. *La Chambre* (1972), *Hotel Monterey* (1972) and *Jeanne Dielman* (1975) contain several aspects of species of spaces relevant to this study. For this purpose, I hypothesize here that filmic everydayness is most prevalent in the home, and that it is possible to establish an architectonic of everydayness in films, concentrating on the home.

Perec's spatial analysis in *Espèces d'espaces* provides us here with our starting point for this investigation. He systematically explores spaces of increasing scale, from the page, the bed, the room...the flat, the building, the street...right up to the universe. Perec starts with the page as, for a writer, this is where the notion of space takes form:

> J'écris : j'habite ma feuille de papier, je l'investis, je la parcours. Je suscite des *blancs*, des *espaces* [...] L'espace commence ainsi, avec seulement des mots, des signes tracés sur la page blanche. Décrire l'espace : le nommer, le tracer [...].[17]
>
> *(Perec, 1974, pp.23,26)*

He carries on with the bed, his bed, which is a source of further spatial exploration: 'J'aime mon lit. J'aime rester étendu sur mon lit et regarder le plafond d'un oeil placide [...] J'aime les plafonds, j'aime les moulures et les rosaces : elles me tiennent souvent lieu de muse'[18] (Perec, 1974, pp.35–36).

Perec continues his spatial investigation by asking a series of questions to define what a bedroom is and how we inhabit it:

> What does it mean, to live in a room? Is to live in a place to take possession of it? What does taking possession of a place mean? As from when does somewhere become truly yours? Is it when you've put your three pairs of socks to soak in a pink plastic bowl? Is it when you've heated up your spaghetti over a camping-gaz? Is it when you've used up all the non-matching hangers in the cupboard? Is it when you've drawing-pinned to the wall an old postcard showing Carpaccio's 'Dream of St Ursula'? Is it when you've experienced there the throes of anticipation, or the exaltations of passion, or the torments of a toothache? Is it when you've hung suitable curtains up on the windows, and put up the wallpaper, and sanded the parquet flooring?
>
> *(Perec, 2008, p.24)*

As it happens, Akerman too shows a fondness for beds, in *La Chambre* (1972), a short, where she is lying on a bed eating an apple, and in *Je tu il elle* (1972), her first feature-length film, where two long 'bed' scenes book-end the film. *La Chambre* is a particularly interesting film from a spatial point of view and the camera movements (shot by Mangolte). It is a filmic

FIGURE 4.3 *La Chambre* (Chantal Akerman, 1972) – stills

exploration of a very ordinary room by a camera centrally placed on a tripod, which rotates anti-clockwise three times, stops at minute seven (out of eleven minutes) and restarts rotating clockwise. The clockwise camera rotation stops again and goes back anti-clockwise a couple more times before the end of the film. The last camera movements are like a pendulum effect, centring on Akerman eating an apple while lying in bed, looking at the camera.

The constant rotation around the room produces the sort of effect that Perec would regard as a form of *dépaysement* [defamiliarization] – making the familiar space an almost abstract space through repetitive techniques of spatial description 'Carry on [making notes] until the scene becomes improbable […] until the whole place becomes strange, and you no longer even know that this is what is called a town, a street, buildings, pavements' (Perec, 2008, p.53). This would be a way of making us rediscover the quotidian in its most banal form and unit: a bedroom. It could also be assimilated to a 'sectional film': as the camera rotates, it slices through the bedroom wall and creates a 'ribbon' effect, or an 'inverted' zoetrope. In *La Chambre*, the everyday in terms of action consists of a woman lying in bed who at some point eats an apple, looking straight at the camera, a rather contemplative act, a singular occurrence in the panoply of domestic routines. But on the other hand the camera invites us to observe around the room a whole range of implied everyday activities pertaining to living in a bedsit. There are dishes in a sink, evidence of food on a table, a kitchen stove with a kettle on it, a writing desk, a cupboard etc. It is a filmed, lived space with the occupant at its centre. It is a succession of a series of moving still lifes. The camera rotations create a room inventory, a visual list of the world in this room. There are no cuts. It's an enumeration of potential everyday activities captured in one single take.

By contrast, in Perec's film *Un homme qui dort* (1974), there are multiple and repeated scenes of everyday life in a tight space (see previous analysis) edited over the space of a year and intercut with city moments. Perec's film constitutes a clinically-observed taxonomy of everydayness, while Akerman's is a rather singular occurrence. Both present different but valuable approaches to film-making everydayness in a single space. Yet another equally useful example of the 'bedroom film' genre is shown in Godard's short, *Charlotte et son Jules* (1958). It's a dialogue – almost a monologue – between a young woman and her former lover (played by Belmondo). She has come back to his bedsit to pick up her toothbrush, and over the course of 12 minutes, Jules lectures her on the errors of her ways. Respecting the unity of time and space, *Charlotte et son Jules* is a light-hearted humorous comedy with a fast-paced dialogue matched by quick cuts. The shooting and editing strategy allows the room to be thoroughly spatially practised by the two protagonists, lying on the bed, sitting on it, sitting at the desk typing, using the sink, opening the French window onto the small street balcony etc. In a short span of time, Godard's film essentially 'speaks' the full vocabulary of the practice of everydayness in that bedroom. There isn't much more that a user of space would be able to demonstrate over and above what's already in this film – the same could also be said of *Un homme qui dort*.

Going up the spatial scale, Perec considers the flat in the following terms:

1. Every apartment consists of a variable, but finite, number of rooms.
2. Each room has a particular function. Apartments are built by architects who have very precise ideas of what an entrance-hall, a sitting-room (living-room, reception room), a parents' bedroom, a child's room, a maid's room, a circulation space, a kitchen, and a bathroom ought to be like. To start with, however, all rooms are alike, more or less, and it is no good their trying to impress us with stuff about modules and other nonsense: they're never anything more than a sort of cube, or let's say rectangular parallelepiped.

(Perec, 2008, p.28)

On the film side, we would struggle to find a better visual text to accompany Perec's writing than *Jeanne Dielman, 23 Quai du Commerce, 1080 Bruxelles*. It stands as a towering giant in the everyday film genre and takes place in an unremarkable series of rectangular parallelepiped volumes.

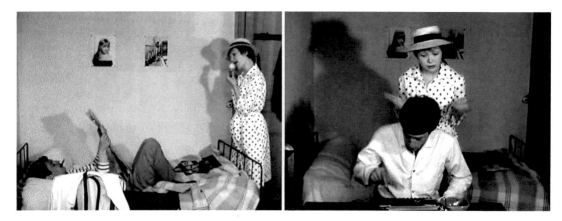

FIGURE 4.4 *Charlotte et son Jules* (Jean-Luc Godard, 1958) – stills